INSPIRING LEGACY

David and Carmen Kreeger's Journey to Philanthropy

SYRIL LEVIN KLINE

Copyright © 2023 The David Lloyd Kreeger Foundation

All rights reserved. No part of this publication in print or in electronic format may be reproduced, stored in a retrieval system, or transmitted in any form or by any means, electronic, mechanical, photocopying, recording, or otherwise without the prior written permission of the publisher.

The scanning, uploading, and distribution of this book without permission is a theft of the author's intellectual property. Thank you for your support of the author's rights.

Design and distribution by Bublish, Inc.
Published by The David Lloyd Kreeger Foundation

ISBN: 9781647046477 (eBook)
ISBN: 9781647046484 (paperback)
ISBN: 9781647046491 (hardcover)

Contents

Foreword v

CHAPTER 1
Breaking New Ground: An Immigrant's Story
Barnet Kreeger (1883–1974) 1

CHAPTER 2
Building Character 14

CHAPTER 3
Life-Changing Courses: Rutgers and Harvard 23

CHAPTER 4
A Love Affair with the Law...31

CHAPTER 5
The New Deal: Excitement in the Air........................42

CHAPTER 6
Love at First Sight 48

CHAPTER 7
European Vacation 1937 60

CHAPTER 8
A Portrait of Carmen 69

CHAPTER 9
    Life Against the Backdrop of History 77

CHAPTER 10
    Cultural Changes in Washington, DC 92

CHAPTER 11
    Karma and Reciprocity 103

CHAPTER 12
    Taking the Plunge into Art 108

CHAPTER 13
    Upheaval, Recovery, and Survival 119

CHAPTER 14
    Breaking Ground: The House That Dared to Be
    More Than a Home 123

CHAPTER 15
    Shakespeare On Trial: The Moot Court 135

CHAPTER 16
    The Shakespeare-Oxfordian Converts:
    An Author's Perspective 143

Epilogue 147
Appendix 153
David Lloyd Kreeger's 75th Birthday Celebration (1984) 161
Gratitude and Acknowledgments 163
Photo Gallery 165
About the Author 187
Index 189

Foreword

by Peter Kreeger and Carol Kreeger Ingall
with Ineke Kreeger and Dr. David Ingall

> Be mindful of your Thoughts - they become your Words.
> Be mindful of your Words - they become your Actions.
> Be mindful of your Actions - they become your Habits.
> Be mindful of your Habits - they become your Character.
> Be mindful of your Character - it becomes your Destiny.
>
> ~ Ancient Chinese Philosopher Lao Tzu

Our parents were extraordinary human beings. As benefactors of the fine and performing arts, their commitment inspired others from all walks of life to appreciate and support the arts. As loving parents and grandparents, they shared their abiding love and respect for all humanity, instilling in us a passion for music, fine arts, literature, and their admiration for the extraordinarily talented and insightful creative artists they met throughout their lives.

David and Carmen were children of immigrants from different cultures who were raised oceans apart. Their parents passed on to them the profound values of education, kindness, honesty, and generosity that served as the foundations of their lives. Both were encouraged to demonstrate their values by treating all people with dignity and respect just as they themselves would want to be treated. This is the great legacy for which we wish them to be remembered.

Fortunately, for us as children, our parents applied reason and maintained a healthy sense of humor while administering these requirements.

Our father once confided that he felt it was his obligation to share the financial results of his success fairly and wisely. This led our parents to follow their hearts to become benefactors of the organizations successfully promoting the arts in Washington, DC.

We often quipped that our parents had more than two children; their extended family included the National Symphony Orchestra, the Washington Performing Arts Society, Arena Stage, the John F. Kennedy Center for the Performing Arts, the Washington Opera, and the National Museum of African Art.

David and Carmen frequently attended the ballet, symphony, theater, and opera. They particularly enjoyed presentations by talented young musicians and artists with the Washington Performing Arts Society and other organizations.

Through charitable contributions, they felt they could best honor and celebrate the brilliant musicians, artists, and performers that they profoundly admired.

Even as they immersed themselves in their philanthropy, our parents led healthy and active lives. Carmen enjoyed dancing, and David danced his way into her heart. Years later, when she and two of her friends discovered Flamenco dancing, they displayed their talents at charitable events. Early in their marriage, David and Carmen often leased horses and rode through Rock Creek Park's meandering trails. Later, they traded their saddles for tennis racquets, which were easier to take along on their vacations. They were avid tennis players and continued playing regularly well into their eighties.

In retrospect, our parents' lives were like a love affair with life: with family, with dear friends, and most importantly with each other. They celebrated almost fifty-three years of marriage before David passed away in November 1990.

An ancient Chinese sage once wrote, "Good fortune is as light as a feather, and few are strong enough to carry it."

We are proud that our parents were among the special few that were strong enough to carry it, and they carried it exceptionally well.

CHAPTER 1

Breaking New Ground: An Immigrant's Story Barnet Kreeger (1883–1974)

> The strangers who reside with you shall be to you as your citizens; you shall love each one as yourself, for you were once strangers in the land.
>
> ~ LEVITICUS 19:33

David Lloyd Kreeger's life of philanthropy would not be complete without including his father's story. Barnet Kreeger, whose friends called him Benny, provided the emotional grounding that rooted David and his siblings in lives of learning and philanthropy.

Barnet was a hardworking man whose courage forged a unique destiny for his children. Like many immigrants, he came to America to escape persecution in his native land, and his efforts allowed future generations of his family to thrive in its climate of freedom.

Fate had carried him through rapidly changing times. Born and raised in Russia, he fled to escape conscription into the Czar's army.

Arriving in London, he worked as a pushcart vendor. Later, after immigrating to the United States, he owned and operated successful grocery businesses in New York and New Jersey. He spent his retirement in Florida, far from his austere beginnings. He reflected on his life in his later years by writing his autobiography. With great foresight, Barnet left his story behind as a time capsule for his descendants so they would know him long after he had passed away.

There is great power in the awareness that one's life story is a legacy worth preserving—a precious family heirloom handed down from one generation to the next, inspiring one's children to understand the personal significance of their own lives in a seemingly impersonal world.

Barnet begins his story with these words:

> I do not remember how old I was when my father died, but I remember well when I and my two brothers came to the *shul*—the synagogue, the House of Prayer—to say *Kaddish*, the memorial prayer, for him. I was so small that they had to stand me up on a bench and a man there said *Kaddish* with me. I still remember well what the man looked like, but I do not remember my father. His inheritance consisted of an unfinished house, which when completed would have been worth 300 rubles, and a closet full of religious books. But my mother, I shall never forget. She was devoted to her children, a very active woman, handy at many things and ready to do any work. After *shiva*, the seven days of mourning as required by Jewish tradition, my mother began planning what to do for a living for herself and the five children. We were three boys and two girls.

Barnet's mother was a rabbi's daughter. She was named Sheine Feige, and her deceased husband had also been a rabbi. According to Jewish tradition, fatherless children were considered orphans even with a widowed mother. As commanded in the Torah, it was (and still is) a moral obligation incumbent upon Jewish communities to provide for widows and orphans through charitable contributions known as *tzedakah*.

Nonetheless, Sheine Feige summoned the determination to become the breadwinner in her family and support her children under tragic and difficult circumstances.

Barnet wrote in his autobiography that he felt that too many of his mother's prayers had gone unanswered, and for that reason, he chose to practice the moral and social justice aspects of Judaism rather than its orthodox rituals. He seems to have given this a great deal of thought, and those were the values he lived by.

Even as a child, he recalled marveling at his mother's strength, character, and courage. He could not have foreseen that years later he would use those same qualities to summon his own courage as a single parent to protect his young family and guide it through the painful circumstances of his wife Laura's progressive illness and death.

Barnet described his hometown of Berdichev as consisting of two perpendicular streets with a few muddy alleyways. He said it had no railway service; horses and wagons were the main transportation. His family's home was across from city hall, and his neighbors included both Jews and gentiles.

After his father's death, his mother opened a bakery that did well for a while but gradually fell on hard times. Barnet recalled that the "pious philanthropist" who had lent her the funds to open the bakery refused to help and seized her late husband's meager possessions as collateral.

"So much for helping widows and orphans," Barnet wrote, with a painful cynicism in his words.

Sheine Feige's sons offered to become laborers to help support the family, but she opposed the idea since it was not related to education or the rabbinate. Barnet's brother Harris apprenticed himself to a bookbinder, a trade that was at least related to education. His brother Nathan pursued religious studies in a *yeshiva* that gave him free room and board so that he was no longer an expense to his family. Barnet remained at home with his mother and two sisters. To help sustain them, he managed horses on a nearby farm.

But even with Nathan living away from home, there was still not enough money to buy the medicine that would have saved Sheine Feige's oldest daughter from death by smallpox. While Barnet did not record her name, he reported that Rose, his younger sister, had survived the illness.

Life became even more complicated in 1902 when Barnet turned seventeen and was required to serve in the Czar's army, an order he could not refuse:

> There was a law in Russia that held parents responsible if their son, who was to be taken into military service, escaped to another country, thus dodging service. A high penalty was imposed on them. The government could, without any notice, come and take away any of their possessions, a house, furniture, even the pillows from the beds, to cover the monetary fine. However, if one escaped after having been drafted and put under military guard, the parent would not be held responsible, and the government had no right to impose the penalty.
>
> I went for conscription, was examined, and declared fit to be a soldier. It was then that I lost my freedom. I did not belong to myself anymore. I was a cog in the Czar's machine. All draftees were sent to a certain district where after a couple of weeks, they were dispatched to different

assignments wherever the military saw fit. It was immaterial to me where I was sent. There was only one thought on my mind—to run away.

Recognizing the legal loophole that would allow his escape, Barnet followed through with the conscription. When he told his mother of his plan, she wept and prayed for God to protect him. He gave her 100 of the 200 rubles he had saved from his work on the farm and kept the rest to enable his escape.

At the military training camp, Barnet often went into town on leave. He would buy several bottles of vodka, not for himself but as a bribe for one of the guards. He encouraged his newfound comrade to arrange even more overnight leave for him. On one occasion, Barnet paid a coachman in advance to take him to the man who would smuggle him out of Russia.

The day of his exodus finally arrived. Barnet went on official leave and never returned to camp. Instead, he hurried to the smuggler, and there he saw a dozen other men who were also fugitives from the army, waiting for the cover of darkness:

> Late at night, he packed us all in a covered wagon like herring in a barrel, and drove us, not telling where. Everyone had to pay his fee in advance. After a few hours of driving, we came to a forest. There was the borderline between Russia and Germany. Normally, the legitimate way of crossing with a passport takes two minutes. Our ordeal took two hours—which seemed like two days. When our wagon approached the forest, a gendarme or perhaps two of them, came seemingly out of nowhere and ordered all of us to get out of the wagon and show our passes. Scared to death, we all got out as ordered. The driver turned to us and shouted in Yiddish,

> "*Chevri!* (My friends!) What are you waiting for? Pick up your legs! Flee! Scram! Run into the woods!"
>
> We all ran, scattering here and there. There was a thick, deep snow on the ground. We could not run far. The gendarmes did not shoot. It appeared that it had been a planned affair with bribes, or the gendarmes surely would have used their guns.
>
> In the forest, a man dressed as a peasant showed up, gathered us together and took us through the woods to an inn, which was in German territory. We all felt tremendously relieved. We lay down for the rest of the night on straw spread on the floor. There we stayed a few days until a boat was ready for London. Before embarking, we were taken to a bathhouse for a health inspection, particularly for the eyes, for trachoma. Thank God, we passed. Of my money, there was enough left for the cheapest ticket with a couple rubles in reserve.

Once he was on the boat, Barnet lost track of time. He felt ill and wasn't sure how long it would take to arrive in London. He left no record of the time, but nevertheless was relieved that he and the others were safe.

Finally, once in London, he spent the rest of his money buying into a pushcart business selling fruits and vegetables:

> One day while pushing the cart loaded with merchandise tied around with strong ropes for security, I had to cross a street where a policeman was directing traffic. Two trams were crisscrossing that intersection. The rails were directly on the street.
>
> The wheels of my cart got caught in the rails and the entire cart was bucked up, with me holding onto the handles, suspended in air. Thanks to the policeman who ran to my

rescue and helped me down, I might otherwise have fallen with my head on the rails, putting me out of commission.

My cart was pulled from the railing and wheeled over to a smooth road. As usual in an accident like that, people gather. My name and place of business were checked, and the story was reported in the newspaper. My friends read about it and came to see me. They urged me to give up such a job, saying it was a job for a common laborer, not for an intelligent fellow like me.

I told them I wanted to work there until I saved sufficient money for a boat ticket to New York. If I could get to a better place, I would make a change. They talked with the boss who promised not to send me on any more deliveries. He kept me busy with work inside the store.

In his autobiography, Barnett said that he wrote a letter to an aunt already living in America and that she sent him a ticket to come by boat. Then, as many immigrants have reported, an American immigration officer misread his papers and officially changed Barnet's last name from "Krugler" to "Kreeger."

There is a far more dramatic tale of Barnet's pushcart accident and how it led to his journey to America. Perhaps he didn't retell it this way because of his own personal modesty, but the story is included here as a family legend for its mythic and almost cinematic qualities.

It begins with Barnet's pushcart stuck on the London tracks. As described earlier, he struggled to free it while others stepped in to help, but the wheels were tightly wedged into the tracks.

The story takes a different turn when, instead of being hoisted high into the air and rescued by a policeman, a frightened horse and buggy bolted uncontrollably toward the cart while the lady inside screamed for help. Everyone leapt out of the way.

But being familiar with horses from his work on the farm, Barnet quickly grabbed the reins and ran with the animal, his boots scraping against the street while he slowed it down. It took a while, but the runaway horse finally stopped. He spoke calmly to reassure it, and having accomplished that, he leaned against the buggy to catch his breath.

The lady in the buggy rested her gloved hand on Barnet's shoulder and thanked him profusely for saving her life. She opened her purse and pulled out a large sum of money, folding his hand around it.

Barnet doffed his cap and thanked her. He replied that anyone would have done the same, but the lady shook her head and pointed out that only he had done so, and that as a hero, he deserved a reward.

It had been a close call, but Barnet's pushcart was finally freed from the tracks and the lady drove on to her destination. Barnet returned home, exhausted.

The legend says that before going to bed, he counted his reward and was astonished to find that there was more than enough money to book his passage to America. There might even be some left over to support himself until he found regular work.

And thus ends the oral history. It's not the one that Barnet recorded, but like most family legends passed down by word of mouth, it had its origin among grateful descendants.

Barnet did write that coming to America had been miracle enough for him. He hadn't known it then, but more miracles were to come.

───── ✦✦✦✦✦ ─────

Soon after arriving in New York, Barnet opened a small grocery store. He quickly found out that life wasn't easy for "greeners," as the newly arrived immigrants were called. One day, he was shocked to discover that he'd run afoul of the law.

A letter had arrived at his shop in a language he did not understand. He innocently showed it to his Hungarian, Romanian, and Polish customers. One woman advised him to throw it away because a boy had written it to her servant girl! Unsure of its contents, Barnet set the letter aside and thought no more about it.

As Barnet wrote in his autobiography, at about nine o'clock that evening, a well-dressed young man entered his shop and asked in English whether he had received a letter for a Miss Frumkin.

Barnet said that a letter had been delivered to him but that he didn't understand it. He had shown it to a few customers and was told the letter was not for him:

> "Here, you can have it." I handed the letter to the man, and he began hollering at me. "What right do you have to open a letter that does not belong to you? You know I can send you to prison for this!" I did not reply. Firstly, I didn't understand what he was talking about. Secondly, I got so scared that I didn't know what to say. The man walked out and soon returned with another man, who said to me, "You're under arrest. Come with me to the police station."

Scared and confused, Barnet reluctantly left the janitor in charge of his shop. He soon worried that the man would forget to lock it up for the night:

> As soon as I entered the police station, they put me behind iron bars like a terrible criminal. I became philosophical. Taking my mother's attitude, I thought, "God will help" and I calmed down. I sarcastically said to myself, now I shall have a chance to sleep a bit. I put my coat under my head and lay

down. I reminded myself that I had left the store unlocked and in the care of the janitor. What shall I do? I didn't see anybody to tell them what happened to me.

At that moment, the door opened. I was told to come out. A man came over and said, "Go home. You must be here tomorrow morning at ten o'clock. The judge will be here."

Barnet found his friends waiting for him when he returned to his store. One woman told him that her son had bailed him out, and that he would represent him in court the next day. She had told her son about the incident and spoke kindly about Barnet, saying that he was a lonely "greener" who was being framed—and after all, he was a good man and a hard worker who had just sent tickets to bring over his entire family from Russia!

In the morning I went to the store as usual, carried breakfast to the customers, stayed in the store until ten o'clock and then went to court, escorted by a dozen men and women like a bridegroom to the altar, some sympathizing, some cracking jokes about the matter.

I felt miserable.

One man said, "A greener is a greener. That man had no right to arrest you. Did he show you a warrant? Did you ask him if he had a warrant? He must have been a friend of the boy, a pimp like him, a make-believe detective."

I didn't even know what a warrant was—or a pimp!

In court, the same young man who had seen me the night before in the police station, came over and showed me where to sit. Then he left.

My turn came. I was sworn in. The judge asked me to tell everything I knew about the matter. In broken English, I told him that the letter was delivered to my address, that I opened it but could not understand it. At that moment, the lawyer handed the judge a paper. After reading it over, the judge said, "Case dismissed."

My lawyer asked me if I wanted to sue the boy and his detective. I said, "No, I don't like to go to court."

On the way back to the store, that boy approached me, showed me a fist and said, "Wait, you are not through with me yet!" Then he walked away.

I thanked the lawyer and asked him to send me a bill. He said I did not owe him anything.

My friends were waiting for me when I returned to the store, and they were happy to see that I was free. Until that event, I did not know how many friends I had in that neighborhood.

In 1905, Barnet sold his store for $500, equivalent to approximately $13,400 today. He bought another grocery store in a busy Polish neighborhood and, after paying off his debts, had $1,100 (approximately $33,000 today) to his name. This, he said, made him feel prosperous enough to propose marriage to Laura Betensky. Barnet left scant details about their wedding, other than to say that Laura was very beautiful and that:

> the marriage ceremony took place at her mother's house. Her mother was very pleased. Firstly, a girl given away in marriage, and secondly, to a man with such good luck.
>
> "He is a millionaire!" she cooed.

Laura worked alongside Barnet in the store. In 1907, she gave birth to their daughter, Shirley. Delighted with the new firstborn, he wrote:

> My wife gave birth to a girl that looked to me like a little angel. Everybody admired the beautiful baby.

And in 1909, David Kreeger was born:

> My dear wife presented me with another child, a boy. He was so pretty that one could not help but love him.

After moving to the Bronx in 1910, the family circle was completed with the birth of Morris. But a few years later, the child became seriously ill. Laura's health also began to decline, and she required occasional hospitalization. Barnet was worried.

> One day, I went in to see how Morris was faring. I took him out of his crib, stood him up and he fell. He could not stand on his feet. He was so weak and emaciated, just skin and bones. He had no strength to talk. I put him back to bed and called the doctor.
>
> The doctor advised, "Mr. Kreeger, there is nothing to lose. We can try taking him out of bed and not put him back. Keep him in your arms, if possible, the whole night. If he falls asleep, let him sleep on your shoulder. I shall come in the morning to see the results."
>
> Imagine how I felt, hearing him say that there is nothing to lose!
>
> I did not sleep that entire night. I held Morris in my arms.
>
> At eight o'clock in the morning the doctor returned, examined Morris, and said, "Well, there is hope."
>
> I felt my heart lighten.

Time passed. Morris survived, and the Kreeger children grew up to pursue their destinies. Morris, who had been so dangerously ill, went on to graduate from medical school and eventually became the executive director of the Michael Reese Hospital in Chicago. In the 1950s, he appointed two African American surgeons to the hospital staff, a controversial and historic first. Barnet was proud to see Morris listed in "Marquis' Who's Who in America."

Shirley married attorney Louis A. Mezey and gave birth to Barnet's first grandchild. Having been diagnosed at the time with a heart condition, Barnet wrote that he was thrilled to have lived to see Freddie's birth.

David became an accomplished violinist and an excellent student. He received a scholarship to Rutgers University and later attended Harvard Law School, where he was editor of the *Harvard Law Review*. Pursuing his career in appellate law during Roosevelt's New Deal, he argued cases on behalf of the Justice Department after previously arguing cases before the Supreme Court. He worked in Puerto Rico for the Puerto Rico Reconstruction Administration (PRRA), where he fell in love with and married Carmen Matanzo. He eventually came upon an interesting business opportunity that changed his life forever. Because of it, he and Carmen became avid art collectors who played important roles in helping to transform sleepy Washington, DC into an active and thriving arts community.

David Lloyd Kreeger picks up the story at this point, but not without some final words from Barnet, written before his passing in 1974:

> Today, my children are, as my mother used to say, "good in the eyes of the people." I cannot say how they seem to God, but with people, I can say they are held in the highest esteem.
>
> I consider myself the happiest man that I have lived to see what is said about my children.

CHAPTER 2
Building Character

> Train up a child in the way he should go and even when he is old, he will not depart from it.
>
> ~ Proverbs 22:6

Every year for the entire summer after school ended, David went on vacation with his mother, Laura; his sister, Shirley; and his brother, Morris, in the Catskill Mountains. The Catskills held a mysterious quality for David since there was always the opportunity to explore new territory. Each summer, Laura chose a different farm or hotel to stay in. Barnet would join his family for a brief respite, returning to the city after a week or so to run his grocery store.

One day, overwhelmed with the spirit of exploration, six-year-old David wandered away from the village. Enchanted by a landscape with a meandering stream, he scaled a nearby hill and surveyed the mountain panorama stretching before him. It was a beautiful day filled with clear mountain air, and the sun was warm and inviting.

Suddenly, he realized that he hadn't told his mother where he was going. He had wandered off without a word! His guilty conscience told him that she would be frantically searching for him everywhere, and that he'd better hurry back.

He returned to the village where a young man reunited him with his mother. Laura opened her purse and rewarded the hometown hero with a quarter.

When David recounted the story years later, he recalled joking with his mother.

"Is that all I was worth to you in those days? Twenty-five cents?"

Modern books on parenting teach that children internalize character traits such as respect, honesty, and empathy by observing the behavior of the adults around them. Good self-discipline is built through observation, practice, and discussion rather than through physical punishment for perceived wrongdoing. Parents can correct hurtful behavior by suggesting better choices that will result in successful relationships and positive resolutions to conflict.

Children can learn that for any given behavior, there are always alternative choices. After all, life is a work in progress.

Long before the existence of books on parenting, Laura and Barnet demonstrated high moral values for their children. Laura, who worked alongside Barnet in the store, always insisted that Shirley, David, and Morris study music and succeed in school. Barnet imbued them with values of excellence, self-respect, and dignity. When Laura became seriously ill and required long periodic hospitalizations, Barnet took on both parental roles, and according to David, did so without complaint. By direct observation of his moral character, Barnet's children received an important and enduring ethical legacy from their father:

We took for granted that all families had the same level of intimacy, warmth, and kindness. It wasn't until later that we were startled to find that it was not the case in every family.

I don't remember my father or mother ever raising a hand to chastise us. But they would punish us if we misbehaved, as all children sometimes do. They would deny us things by way of a punishment, but they were very kind and loving.

My father had a concept that no one has the right to hurt another person's feelings. He would watch us sometimes with our peers and with older people. Even at the slightest hint of carelessness or thoughtlessness in saying or doing something that might hurt another person, my dad would stop us and call it to our attention. He made it very important for us to consider the feelings of others.

I think that gave all three of us children an inner self-assurance.

Like most immigrants seeking success in the United States, Barnet had to start from scratch to build economic security for his family. He maintained a reputation as an honest businessman and had faith that doing so would lead to prosperity. David was heavily influenced by his father's example and found that hard work was truly quite enjoyable:

My sister Shirley and I were born when our parents lived on 12th Street in Greenwich Village. My brother was born after we moved to the Bronx. I recall those days with nostalgia because my dad was doing reasonably well for an immigrant. He owned his own grocery store on 152nd Street. He had a horse and buggy, and we would drive out to Westchester, which was wild country then. One hundred years ago, it took an hour and a half to get there from where we lived! We would pick corn from the stalk and harvest fresh tomatoes, lettuce, and cucumbers, and we'd have a picnic in the buggy. We would use that buggy to go to the market and buy fresh eggs and butter, which he would sell in his little grocery store. Those were such wonderful days.

When David was nine years old, Laura encouraged him to study the violin, hoping that he would one day become a professional musician. David enjoyed his regular lessons, but when he found that one of his teachers was particularly harsh and demanding, he devised a resourceful way of dealing with it:

> Each time I made a mistake, the violin teacher would rap my knuckles with the bow. I would cry through half the lesson! Sadly, I didn't always have enough time to practice, and teachers were very demanding of their students back then. I would do part of a lesson but sometimes I couldn't finish it, and I would need to practice for two hours just to be ready for the next lesson the following week. That's why I decided to become a very good sight-reader, so that I could avoid those whacks with the violin bow! I ended up developing a good aptitude for sight-reading, which stands me in good stead in our chamber music sessions.

David never abandoned his love for the violin, but he decided against becoming a professional musician. He felt humbled by the constant practice and complete devotion required by professionals. Barnet suggested that he pursue a career in business, which would ensure him a solid livelihood. David agreed, and eventually chose to study law.

As the years passed, David's successful legal career enabled his philanthropic support of the arts, which stemmed from his ardent respect for those who devoted their entire lives to practicing and perfecting their art. He encouraged many young students and aided their careers by sponsoring competitions, prizes, and awards.

Although not a professional violinist, David was considered a well-practiced amateur who played for the sheer love of it. He was most happy when playing chamber music in his home with his good friends Sidney and Faith Forrest and Supreme Court Justice Abe Fortas, one of his former coworkers at the PRRA.

Beyond a doubt, his mother would have been very proud.

Sometimes the younger generation is forced to learn life's lessons the hard way. Even David, who performed so well scholastically in elementary and junior high school that he eventually skipped two grades, had the *chutzpah* to express his opinion on paper about one of his teachers.

Being a clever cartoonist requires skillful drawing, a lively sense of humor, and sardonic wit. David had these qualities in excess, but his teacher wasn't amused:

> When I was in the fourth grade, I used to bring home straight A's on my report card. Students were graded with three marks in those days: one for the basics like reading, spelling and arithmetic, and then a mark for conduct, and lastly, a mark for effort.
>
> Well, it happened that for the first time in three or four years, I brought home a report card with two A's and a B+. The B+ was in conduct, and my father was very upset.
>
> It all happened because I had begun to draw, and I drew an unflattering caricature of my teacher.

As punishment, David's teacher made him sit in front of the class on a high stool and announced with pedagogical severity that this was the consequence of ill-advised creativity:

> I was nine or ten-years-old, and when I showed my father my report card, I remember him asking, "Why? What happened?" Normally, most parents would have been happy with A, B+, A. But my father was very upset because he had been accustomed to seeing three A's all the time.
>
> His standards were very rigorous. He wasn't a cruel man by any means, but he was an exacting man, and he made it clear to us that we were all expected to live up to fairly high standards, and that education was important.

David brought his grade back up the following term. He may have drawn other caustic cartoons of teachers over the years, but he confessed that the report card experience taught him to be a little more guarded about leaving his caricatures unattended.

When David was eleven years old, Barnet sold his grocery store and invested in the milk pasteurization and bottling business. He wrote:

> With a few partners, my father bought three creameries: one in New Brunswick and two in Pennsylvania. They bought milk from farmers, pasteurized and bottled it, and sold it in the north New Jersey market, in Jersey City and Newark.
>
> Since one of the creameries was located in New Brunswick, we moved to the suburb of Highland Park. We lived on a tree-lined street with colorful leaves falling in the autumn. It was the first time we'd ever seen anything like that! The woods were two blocks away, and we'd gather

chestnuts in the fall. It was really beautiful, being suddenly plunged into a semi-rural atmosphere.

I skipped two grades in the New York public schools and attended junior high school when I was twelve. I graduated from high school when I was sixteen, in 1925.

In high school, David became a public speaker, a master of ceremonies, and a toastmaster of sorts. He refined his material by giving speeches at assemblies. He memorized stories from joke books and adapted them for school situations.

The only downside to this "gig" was that the members of a high school fraternity he had pledged demanded that he stop, believing it was inappropriate for the fourteen-year-old to be seen as a comedian.

That didn't bother David, who enjoyed the spontaneity of being a raconteur. He thrived on audience feedback and liked to think fast on his feet.

David decided to combine his performance skills with his spirit of generosity to make a difference at school. He formed a violin quartet with some friends to raise money for the school's athletic field. The quartet played several concerts, and audiences bought tickets for general admission. On good nights they earned thirty dollars, and they contributed every penny of it to the athletic fund.

But not all of David's turns in the spotlight were easy. He recalled the time he suffered from a serious case of stage fright:

> I was the concertmaster in my high school orchestra, and they asked me to play a solo for Music Week. I was about fifteen or sixteen then, and it was before I graduated.
>
> I played Pablo de Sarasate's *Zigeunerweisen* and suddenly had a temporary memory lapse. I stopped playing in the

middle of the performance, and the pianist stopped because obviously I had lost my way.

The music teacher, a rather excitable elderly man, stood in the wings and said in a hoarse whisper, "My God! My God! What are you doing?"

I walked offstage and told him I forgot the music.

"What are you going to do now?" he asked.

There was a hush in the audience. Then there were gasps, and you could hear sympathetic murmurings of "oh, poor fellow."

Again, my teacher asked me what I was going to do.

"I'm going to go back out there and try it again," I told him.

I walked back and pointed to a bar about ten measures back from where I had stopped, to a place where I saw something familiar. I finished the piece to great applause, probably because the audience knew that it took tons of courage to go back out there.

To this day, I don't know where I got the courage after leaving the stage to the horror of the music teacher, when all I wanted to do was to hide for the rest of my life.

Laura became seriously ill in the late 1920s. Even with the onset of her illness, David recalled his mother's sense of joy and adventure.

> We'd walk up and down the boardwalk at Atlantic City and buy saltwater taffy and ride in those rolling chairs. It was wonderful!
>
> But my mother became ill, and it was a traumatic experience. Sometimes she was so weak, she could barely move. She wasn't a strong person, and she would have to be away

from us for a week or two at a time in the hospital. When that happened, my father took on both parental roles, but we never heard him complain about it.

My mother died when she was forty-one. My father never remarried. Perhaps my mother's succession of illnesses made him feel that another marriage would divert his attention away from raising the three of us children.

Whatever his reasoning, he devoted himself to us wholeheartedly. He showed no signs of bitterness, resentment, or a desire to escape. He set an example of kindness, wisdom, and moral strength that none of us have ever forgotten.

Psychologists have studied the significance of a surviving parent's attitude after the death of a spouse. How that parent responds after the event makes a profound difference in the child's recovery. Like the push and pull of the ocean's tides, the ebb and flow of grief must be processed. The idea of working through the trauma is very real.

Barnet seems to have understood the skills of effective parenting long before the existence of professional counseling, but neither he nor David left behind any personal details of their emotional struggles with Laura's illness and death.

Life goes on and time forces families to adjust.

Perhaps the violin eased David's grief over his mother's death. Laura had passed her love for music down to him, giving him the gift of a lifetime.

CHAPTER 3

Life-Changing Courses: Rutgers and Harvard

The way we see the future has everything to do with how well we can look up and see the expanded horizon before us.

~ PETER LEE KLINE, AUTHOR AND EDUCATOR

David graduated from high school with honors when he was sixteen years old and was awarded a full scholarship to Rutgers University. Sadly, his mother had to be hospitalized at the time and was unable to celebrate his achievements with the rest of the family.

Nevertheless, Laura and Barnet had profoundly impressed on their children the importance of education. David valued learning through college and law school, and throughout the course of his lifetime. In his later years, he spoke about how the study of law sharpens clarity and critical thinking:

> In almost every walk of life, I have found that one can deal with situations more effectively when he or she has had the benefit of legal training. When someone asks me

a question, my wife Carmen says that the first thing I do is cross-examine them. That's because sometimes the question that is asked is based on an inadequate presentation of the facts, and if you answer that question using only the pre-selected facts, you may be giving the wrong advice. Before I make a judgment, I want to know the entire periphery of all the facts and issues. When you study the law, you are taught how to do that, and you must have all of that in front of you before going on to the principles. That kind of training sharpens a person's reasoning.

David also believed that studies in science, music, art, and history increase vital critical thinking skills. He recognized that Socratic inquiry is a large part of the learning process. While the study of law could teach a person the basics of reasoning, inquiry wasn't reserved simply for ascertaining the facts of a case. He believed that students who wanted to learn any subject could use the process of inquiry to hone their thinking skills, and he practiced that technique often.

He would have disapproved of schools teaching to the test and removing art and music from their curricula, leading students to learn only how to parrot back lecture notes and desired exam responses. David understood that when creative abilities are encouraged and exercised, the brain's neurological pathways grow and increase human performance. This brand of excellence was very important to David.

While attending Rutgers University, David illustrated a variety of cartoons for the college magazine:

> I started out as an assistant art editor, and then became the chief art editor of the *Rutgers Chanticleer*, a humor magazine.

> It was subsequently suppressed for a double-entendre joke that today would not even have titillated a pre-teenager. But the magazine was censored in those days, even though it was a wonderful publication. I drew cartoons and some were reprinted in *College Humor*, a magazine anthology that published jokes and cartoons from various college papers. Drawing led me towards an interest in draftsmanship, etching and the ability to create an object or character with line and color.

And then, of course, there was music:

> I played in the instrumental clubs and that was a very nice part of my college years. There was the Rutgers Glee Club and the Rutgers Instrumental Club, and they traveled together to other colleges like Amherst and Smith. When we performed, there would be a dance afterwards. It was perfectly proper to "cut in," to tap the man who was dancing with a lovely girl and then dance with her yourself. We made many friendships that way. We were all dressed like penguins in black tie, and we were all about the same age. There was the glamor of having been performers. The girls had just seen and heard us, and we were walking on air. It was a wonderful experience that I enjoyed immensely.

David was a political science major when he registered for a course that was destined to change his life. He reflected his enthusiasm for Dr. Thomas Munro's art history class in his recorded memoirs, interviews, and speeches:

The History of Art course began with the Byzantine period and went through the early Renaissance, Giotto and Duccio, and into the high Renaissance with Bellini, Veronese, Tintoretto and Titian. It then moved into the 17th century with Rembrandt and the Dutch masters, and then to the 18th century portraitists, the English and Venetians, Caneletto and Guardi. From then on, we studied the 19th century and the Academic School, the Impressionists and post-Impressionists and then the Paris school with Picasso and Miró. En route there was a view of African art and its influence on the twentieth century contemporary scene, and an in-depth study of Cezanne. It was a marvelous course! Everybody in that class was imbued with an understanding, respect, and love for great art. Maybe they didn't all become collectors, but I'm sure it broadened their understanding and enjoyment of trips to museums or seeing art in a home or gallery.

Even as a cartoon illustrator, David expanded his understanding of representational art through Munro's class. The professor's fresh approach to collective and individual art appreciation was considered revolutionary in its time:

> In Munro's course on Philosophy and Aesthetics, we studied why people enjoy looking at paintings beyond the fact that the subject matter might evoke memories or recollections of a similar scene. That's only a secondary aspect of art. You could do that with a photograph or a poor painting that just shows a barn at the edge of a stream. But what is it that makes a painting great? Munro analyzed that. First there is the visual response; secondly, the emotional response. Professor Munro showed us that a response could also apply to a nonrepresentational painting like an abstraction, or even

a surrealistic painting, which had nothing at all to do with reality. I attribute Professor Munro's two courses for the consuming interest I share with my wife Carmen in collecting and living with great paintings.

Munro took his students on museum visits to encourage their appreciation of a variety of styles and techniques. His class once visited the Barnes Foundation, the private collection founded in 1922 outside Philadelphia. When David innocently asked Munro why so few people were there to see the masterpieces, the professor hastily shushed him. Munro, who had served as the museum's associate director of education, explained that his friend, art collector Dr. Albert C. Barnes, and Barnes's mentor, the honorary educational director John Dewey, believed that the experiential study and discussion of great works of art enabled students to develop high-order critical thinking skills. But while Barnes considered students to be interested observers, he feared that the general public would loiter, damage, and destroy his art collection. That, Munro explained, was why Barnes had restricted public access to his exhibition to just two days a week.

Many years later in response to legal challenges, the Barnes Foundation opened its doors to the public in 1961, admitting no more than five hundred people at a time for two and a half days a week. Members of the public were required to schedule by appointment two weeks in advance. These restrictions did not apply to university students who regularly visited with their classes.

Another positive influence on David at Rutgers was Professor William Kirk, an Oxford-educated Englishman who taught Latin. David had already completed four years of Latin in high school. In his sophomore year at Rutgers, he studied Latin poetry, Livy's books about the Punic Wars, and other ancient works with Professor Kirk.

At the end of that year, David asked Professor Kirk what advanced courses he would be teaching next year. Kirk said he wouldn't be teaching any, since none of the students seemed interested in advanced Latin. He added that he had once taught a course in Roman law, but that class was dropped due to lack of student interest. Undaunted, David asked Professor Kirk how many students he would need to teach Roman law, and he responded that he would need at least fifteen. David swung into action and lobbied his friends to sign up for the course:

> I just wanted to study with Professor Kirk. He was a marvelous man—so inspiring, so learned, so eloquent, a true gentleman with a depth of scholarship. It was a pleasure to sit and listen to him talk about any subject. I decided to round up fifteen of my friends and browbeat them into taking the course. I told them that it was going to be an easy bread-and-butter course, and what a wonderful man Professor Kirk was. My fifteen friends signed up and the professor agreed to give the course. It was listed in the curriculum. But then in September, five of my friends got cold feet and changed to some other subjects, and then I only had ten. Professor Kirk didn't seem to mind. He told me that because of my enthusiasm, he was going to teach the course anyway. Professor Kirk's course on Roman law opened my eyes to the marvels of the law. It's a little different than our common law but in principle, it's not too far different. I'm certain that course led me to law school.

David's respect for Professors Munro and Kirk is remarkable since most students rarely analyze their professors' methods for teaching new information. Some professors find that kind of analysis threatening, as did one undergraduate instructor whose lectures alienated David and the entire class:

> There was a Constitutional Law instructor who would justify every Supreme Court decision whether it was expressly overruled or not, no matter how inconsistent it was with another decision. He would say it could be reconciled and give some minor, trivial, or irrelevant point of distinction. We got into some heated arguments about some of the Civil War cases, the Dred Scott decision, and the slaughterhouse cases. Some were overruled, some were not, but the Supreme Court would deftly avoid any inconsistent precedent. Still, this teacher would justify it rather than say there was a change in the personnel of the Court, or in the social or political times or in the perception of some critical issues of the day that would influence the Court.

When David challenged the instructor, he was reprimanded and kept after class. The instructor asked David why he insisted on making his life so hard, and David responded that he wasn't trying to do that. Nevertheless, there were consequences for challenging the instructor:

> "I am the professor here, not you," he said. And he gave me a C– for the course. He called one of my friends and said, "Talk to him. Tell him to get off my back or I'm going to flunk him." My friend said, "He's going to be Phi Beta Kappa. He gets all A's." "He does?" replied the instructor. "I don't believe it." "Yes, he does," my friend said. "He's one of the top men in the class." I ended up graduating third in the class, or something like that, even with that C–. In any event, it was an interesting experience, and it taught me that sometimes you pay the price when you don't conform or play the game, but you do feel better about speaking up.

In 1929, David graduated *magna cum laude* from Rutgers. He continued his studies at Harvard Law School and indulged his love for art and music by visiting galleries and attending concerts. Like many Bostonians, he bought discount tickets at the Friday Afternoon Rush to hear Serge Koussevitzky conduct the Boston Symphony Orchestra, often sitting so high up and far away from the stage that he could *hear* the orchestra playing but not actually *see* it. Back then, David couldn't have foreseen that one day he would welcome such greats as Isaac Stern, Pinchas Zukerman, Mstislav Rostropovich, and many other musical luminaries to his magnificent home on Foxhall Road, surrounded by original paintings of Monet, Renoir, van Gogh, Cézanne, Chagall, Picasso, Miró, and Kandinsky.

That future was still a work in progress.

CHAPTER 4

A Love Affair with the Law

The law is the true embodiment of everything that's excellent.

~ WILLIAM S. GILBERT, LAWYER AND SATIRIST

David credited Professor Kirk's Roman law course for igniting his interest in a legal career. Oddly enough, he also credited the poorly taught constitutional law course for the same reason.

To paraphrase Charles Dickens, David believed that "it was the best of courses, it was the worst of courses." The poorly taught course required his constant questioning of the instructor's awkward and misleading presentations. Because he never shied away from an intellectual challenge, and because he put some effort into interpreting those classes, it worked to David's benefit. He was drawn toward the clarity and mental discipline required by legal reasoning.

It was a career match made in heaven.

Earlier, as a student at Highland Park High School, David had also excelled at algebra, solid geometry, and trigonometry. He liked that in each of these disciplines, one could get as close to an absolute answer as possible, in stark contrast with real-life experiences, where most problems don't have clear-cut, one-size-fits-all solutions.

Critical thinking was at the crux of David's love affair with the law. It was the perfect blend of reasoned, left-brained, concrete logic and right-brained abstraction and situational variations. Given axioms of specific legal principles in a case, their application to the facts was, and still is, a matter of logic and reason.

Professor Munro opened the door to David's love of art and aesthetics. While the law dealt with issues and conflicts between ordinary people as well as business, government, and social relationships, it was completely unconcerned with philosophy, ideas, and abstractions:

> When you invest the legal situation with human values, you're in a gray area. That's why you will have the highest court in the land disagree on important issues and you'll have a five to four decision with the dissenting opinions being just as persuasive as the majority opinion. At the time of my study, it seemed to me that I was in a realm of clarity and purity of mind, and that appealed to me. I also found myself drawn to the logicality and application of reason to problems, and that most of them dealt with real down-to-earth situations.

As it turned out, Harvard was the *only* law school to which David had applied, and even in the late 1920s that was quite a gamble. However, being accepted into Harvard back then was not difficult. All one needed was a college diploma:

> This was in 1929, when we were still riding high before the bubble burst on Wall Street in October. It was about April or May of 1929 when I started the application process, perhaps even a few months earlier, and the replies were encouraging. I

found that when I got to campus, the captain of the Rutgers water polo team, a wonderful man, was there too. I think he averaged a C– and had gotten through Rutgers by the skin of his teeth. But there he was at Harvard.

From there, the brutal process of elimination, reminiscent of a scene from the 1973 film *The Paper Chase*, began. While David noted that anyone with a college diploma could be admitted to Harvard Law School in 1929, many students were brutally cast out during the first year:

> In the very first week, I think it was in the torts class, the professor said, "Look to the right and look to the left. At the end of the year, some of you will be gone." That was no exaggeration. They flunked from 30 percent to 40 percent of the freshman class in the first year. And then in the second year, they would flunk another 15 percent to 20 percent, so that actually perhaps 50 percent to 55 percent of the class would graduate. Now, that was a very wasteful and cruel system. Today it doesn't prevail. They screen the applicants so carefully and the standards of admission are so exacting and so high that you must have virtually a straight A average to get into Harvard Law School, and the result is that only a miniscule percentage flunk out.

Some who flunked out didn't bother to tell their parents, but simply transferred to other nearby law schools. Then, according to David, they took the subway to Cambridge and mailed letters home from there, as if nothing had happened.

While David was an excellent student, he admitted by the end of his first year that he was not always sure how well he had done. There was no way to know for certain until after finals. Midyear mock and trial exams didn't count, and students were never told whether their grades were good or bad:

> After the final examinations, I made the mistake of joining a postmortem at the rooms of three or four of my friends and found that my answers were diametrically opposite from theirs! I knew that when I got back home to New Brunswick, my friends would ask, "Well, how did you like Harvard Law School?" And to protect myself, to give myself a golden bridge of retreat, I would say, "Well, it was all right, but I'm not sure if I'm going back next year." I wanted to keep my retreat as graceful as possible. I fully expected to get bad marks. I almost jumped through the ceiling when I got a letter telling me I made Law Review! I thought somebody was pulling my leg! It turned out that Harvard worked on a very sound principle: the answer to questions didn't matter. You could say "liability" or "no liability," you could say "judgment for the plaintiff" or "judgment for the defendant," you could say "guilty" or "not guilty"; it didn't matter. The reasoning—how you arrived at the conclusion—was the only important thing, and if your reasoning was persuasive and showed that you had absorbed the fundamentals of the principles and cases you'd had to study, you could do well even if the professor disagreed with your conclusion.

In the 1930s, Harvard maintained an admission quota that did not favor Jews. Its quota was based on the bizarre assumption that Jewish students had certain characteristics that would be objectionable to the majority; therefore, if there weren't too many Jews on campus, there would be no anti-Semitism, and Jews would not be exposed to overt hostility and possible danger at Harvard.

David said many times that he personally did not feel discriminated against at Harvard, although he found the social distance between Jews and non-Jews very divided. He graduated *magna cum laude* from Harvard Law School in 1932, and although he hadn't personally experienced anti-Semitism on campus, he faced it in the job market.

No one had warned him that the leading law firms in New York, Chicago, and other large cities did not want Jewish lawyers:

> One would usually start interviewing in January and February, with the greatest activity happening during the Easter holidays. When I went to New York in the Spring of 1932, I was simply told, "Oh, here's the list of the big law firms." I had been on the Law Review, and theoretically, all of the firms wanted Law Review men. If you were a gentile Law Review man, you could practically pick your law firm; they all wanted him. I went through the gamut. There was one very large law firm where I passed hurdles one and two, the interviewing partner and one of the senior partners. Then I got to the top man, who was the very first name in the law firm, and he looked at me narrowly and coldly. He didn't ask me my religion, but he asked me a good deal about my interests and activities. I told him I played the violin and had become a jazz pianist. "Well," he said, "what about when you were at college? Did you play football? Did you do this? Did you do that?" Little by little he was beginning to type me. And then he said, "Now, Kreeger. What kind of a name is that? It sounds German."

David replied that his father came from Russia and that the name had originally been Krugler, but an immigration inspector changed it to Kreeger by misreading the *u* for two *e*'s and dropping the *l* completely:

They had been so taken with me. They asked me what articles I had written when I was on the Law Review. I told them, and they were very impressed. I got along beautifully with them. I thought I had the job. I was very confident because the second hurdle, which was one of the senior partners, said, "Yes, we like what you've done, and we think that there might be a place for you." He mentioned the corporate law department or something that related to one of the articles I had written. The head of the firm couldn't see me until later in the day, so I went to lunch and phoned my Dad, and told him I thought I had a job with the biggest firm on Wall Street! Then I phoned one of my law school friends in New York and told him about it. I thought I had the job! I even went to the barber and had a shave. I was so elated, so exhilarated about the prospect, and wanted to put on my best appearance for the senior partner. When I went back, the second person greeted me very cordially. "Oh yes. I'm going to take you to Mr. So-and-So" and he took me in. Well, within about ten minutes, I began to sense that the temperature had dropped about twenty degrees. He was a very fine man, one who held high federal office, but obviously the firm didn't want to hire Jews.

Unlike modern equal opportunity hiring practices, it was not against the law to inquire about one's religion in those days. Anti-Semitism was frequent and by no means secret or subtle:

> There was another firm where they asked me outright, "What is your religion, Mr. Kreeger?" and I said, "I'm Jewish." He squirmed and said, "Well, we have no prejudices here, but many of our clients don't like to deal with Jewish lawyers, and I hope you'll understand that as a matter of business, we just don't hire Jewish lawyers in our firm." This was not

one of the giants, but it was a very sizeable firm with fifty or sixty lawyers. As a matter of fact, there were law firms where they had one or two Jewish partners. It would be mixed, and there were well-known law firms where they hired very few Jews because it was true that in dealing at the highest corporate levels in those days, there were very few Jews, if any. Some might have risen to manager of a division or assistant vice president, but they virtually had no chance of getting to the top. Consequently, there was a feeling on the part of many law firms that "We'd better play it safe, and since we have a roster of gentile clients, we'd better give them gentile lawyers to deal with."

While David didn't believe that Jews were better lawyers than anyone else, he knew that the social barriers of discrimination and exclusion caused all minority candidates to work harder:

I don't think that you can overlook the fact that when you're reared in an atmosphere of exclusion and discrimination, when you feel that there is a barrier between you and the majority of the population, there are some psychological debts you have to pay. I think for that reason back then, Jewish lawyers had to try harder.

David clarified his expectations. He was ultimately offered a position with a mixed but predominantly Jewish law firm in New York City. His friend Nat Jacobs suggested that he consider a smaller firm in Newark, which had three partners and seven or eight lawyers. That firm was also closer to David's home in New Brunswick. He recalled that:

Nat said, "Why go to the large firm? You'll only be one man out of fifty or sixty, and you'll be working very hard with lots of overtime. It's like a factory, commuting to New

York. Newark is closer and the firm is smaller, and there'll be more of a chance for you." I agreed with his reasoning, so I accepted the job with the small firm in Newark. It was about a 45 minute commute on the Pennsylvania Railroad from New Brunswick, and I worked there for two years. And Nat was right! It was a very wonderful learning experience, plus the fact that the 45 minutes on the train each way permitted me to do more reading than I had done over any prior comparable period of time. I read completely through Shakespeare and the Russian novelists Dostoyevsky, Turgenev and Tolstoy. I was a fast reader in those days. There would be a bridge game going on across the aisle from me with a number of my friends, but I didn't join them. I wanted to read. It was a marvelous period of time.

David was the only *Law Review* man at the Newark firm, which gave him a position of "almost oracular importance." This came about when a larger New York firm, at the request of its wealthy banking and insurance clients, wanted to hire him to study World War I veterans' benefits, which it felt the government was too generously overpaying:

> The firm questioned the definition of a veteran. A man who was a paper-pusher and only did some clerical work in the war would get a heart attack or diabetes or kidney failure, and then was sent to a hospital at government expense, or he would start receiving a disability pension, and so on. The clients thought that maybe we ought to concentrate on the active-duty men, the real soldiers who had been on the front lines. The whole idea was to save money for the government, of course. Well, I didn't like the assignment, so I turned it down. I had no real sympathy with it or the direction it was going.

David had been with the Newark firm for a year and a half when Franklin D. Roosevelt was elected president of the United States in the autumn of 1932. Roosevelt's inauguration took place in 1933, and by the end of that year, the New Deal had begun.

David was offered a job in Washington. The offer came when he was asked to write a brief for the Court of Appeals of New Jersey that represented its position on whether a tax judgment of the New York courts should be given full faith and credit in the New Jersey courts:

> There is a clause in the Constitution that says in effect that the public acts and records of one state shall have the same effect in other states as they have in the state in which they've been rendered. This means that if you get a legal judgment in New York and the defendant lives in Illinois, you don't have to try that case over again in Illinois. In the United States, the Constitution says all courts are equal. In the case I argued, here was a tax that a corporation hadn't paid to the State of New York, which obtained a judgment in the New Jersey courts. I wrote a brief for the Court of Appeals, and we sued on the judgment in the New Jersey courts saying that we were entitled to full faith and credit because this company had assets in New Jersey. We wanted to attach those assets to pay the tax judgment, and I argued that.
>
> All the earlier statements that had said you don't have to enforce tax judgments are *obiter dictum*, meaning that it has never been decided. Besides, it has no real justification in fairness or equity or even in law to deny it because the Constitution says full faith and credit must be given. True, the courts have said, "Well, we're not going to enforce the criminal judgments of another state." Okay, but we were not talking about a criminal judgment. We were talking about a

debt. These people didn't pay the taxes they were supposed to have paid.

We won in the Fourth Court of Appeals. This was a landmark case in New Jersey, so I was invited to talk about it in Washington early in 1934.

David traveled to Washington and appeared before a panel of twenty-five editors under the auspices of the Judicial Conference of Senior Judges of the Courts of Appeals on the restatement of the law on conflicts. There were judges; scholars; professors of law from Chicago, Pennsylvania, Harvard, and Yale; and one or two practicing lawyers evaluating his case. David argued why it was right and why the case cited by Joey Beale, his former professor at Harvard, was distinguishable:

> It was a statement made by a lower court, which was reversed by the appellate court on other grounds, so the highest court never ruled on that point, and the lower court that had ruled on it said that by the way of *obiter dicta*, it had nothing to do with the decision. Therefore, it was the weakest kind of authority and they all recognized it.
>
> But since Professor Beale had been teaching for years that you don't give full faith and credit to tax judgments, he hated to have his statement changed so he held out against it. It took the second or third edition before they finally revised it to suit the law.
>
> Now it wasn't binding on anybody, it was just a restatement expressing the opinion of experts, but it acquired a great deal of weight, and lawyers will cite the restatement in their legal briefs. Even judges will cite restatement of law as an authority in the footnotes of their opinions.

During David's 1934 visit to Washington, he met with several classmates who had already moved there to assume leadership roles in the "alphabet agencies" of President Roosevelt's New Deal. They lived in small groups of two or three, worked seven days a week, twelve hours a day, and loved it. The idea of joining them was very appealing.

Within a month of his presentation before the Judicial Conference, David accepted a job with the federal government.

His law partners in Newark had warned him against it. His colleagues said:

> "You'll be ruined. You'll become a bureaucrat. You'll become a wage slave. You'll become a clock-watcher. Here you have a great future. Someday, who knows, you might even become a junior partner and earn five thousand a year."

Nonetheless, intrigued by the New Deal, David accepted a job in the Legal Division of the Agricultural Adjustment Administration. He was so well respected at his Newark firm that it offered him one year's leave of absence just in case things in Washington didn't work out.

But without looking back, David embraced a new life in the nation's capital, where a future of art, music, enduring treasured friendships, and romance awaited him.

CHAPTER 5

The New Deal: Excitement in the Air

> Let us never forget that government is ourselves and not an alien power over us. The ultimate rulers of our democracy are not a president and senators and congressmen and government officials, but the voters of this country.
>
> ~ President Franklin D. Roosevelt

In 1934, David began playing his part in President Roosevelt's New Deal:

> Many of my classmates were already in Washington, and they loved what they were doing. They were working twelve hours a day, seven days a week. There was a real excitement in the air! They felt that they were part of a revitalization of our country, of our economy, and it's hard to describe the enthusiasm and effervescence that existed then. People were devoted so wholeheartedly to their jobs. They were sure they were saving the country and the world. It was a heady experience that you would never find in a law firm.

INSPIRING LEGACY

David began his career at the Agricultural Adjustment Administration (AAA), working alongside Jerome Frank as general counsel and Francis Shea as assistant counsel. He had met Shea earlier that year when making his presentation before the Judicial Conference of Senior Judges of the Courts of Appeals. At the time, Shea roomed with Telford Taylor, one of David's Harvard classmates. Taylor is best known for his role as a member of the prosecution at the Nuremberg Trials and as an outspoken critic of Senator Joseph McCarthy in the 1950s. Taylor also became a vocal critic of American policy during the Vietnam War in the 1960s.

The AAA was first tasked with supervising the reduction of agricultural crops, which had reached such great abundance during the Depression that prices had fallen very low. Because of this, farmers suffered serious economic hardship. At that time in our nation's history, generations of family farmers, rather than the corporate agricultural conglomerates of today, were growing the bulk of America's food supply. Congress opted to alleviate the farmers' problem by supporting crop reduction and paying farmers for acreage not planted rather than offering them direct financial subsidies for growing specific crops. David personally felt a better plan would have included accommodating the storage of excess grain, cotton, and tobacco to meet future demands.

As a member of its legal division, David wrote opinions on behalf of the AAA for the program. In the course of his work, however, a dramatic controversy erupted. General counsel Jerome Frank, assistant general counsel Lee Pressman, and John Abt, who was head of the Litigation Section, were all suddenly dismissed. Shea and others were also drawn into the controversy, which had erupted along racial and economic lines between farmers and sharecroppers:

The issue arose as to whether benefit payments made to the farmer, who was reducing his cotton production, should also go to the sharecropper. Ninety-five percent of the sharecroppers were Black, and they were the ones who were actually raising the cotton. Under that system, the sharecroppers were in a very difficult position because they rarely received cash for their share of the crop. They would purchase necessities at a company store where prices were fixed by the owner of the farm. I won't say that all of the farmers were dishonest, but in some cases, they overreached and charged the sharecropper more than the going price for the food that they bought. Sometimes the farm owners made cash advances to the sharecroppers. The result was that usually at the end of the planting season, the farmers would tell the sharecroppers that their bill at the company store and the amount of money advanced them during the year was equal to their share of the crop, so they got nothing but the reduction of their debt. There were cases where there were 300 acres, and the sharecropper would get anywhere from one-third to one-half of the crop, based on his agreement with the farmer. If he supplied his own implements and his own cutting and harvesting tools, he would get one-half. If he just lived on the premises and only did manual work, he might get as little as one-fourth or one-third.

With millions of dollars being paid out to cotton farmers who had reduced their planting, the AAA wrote a provision into the agreement requiring that sharecroppers also receive a portion of the subsidy because the reduction in crops also reduced their share:

> There was no doubt that that's what was intended in the contract, but the question arose as to the policing of that provision. Could the AAA enforce it, or must that be left

to the local authorities in a small parish or county court, which was dominated by the farmers? The farmers took the position that they should decide how much the sharecropper gets, and that Washington shouldn't interfere with that; it was none of their business.

David prepared a legal opinion, which held that all the payments to farmers could be suspended if there were verified complaints from sharecroppers that they were not receiving their fair share:

> The landowners were irate at that because they said, "We'll decide what they get, and if they don't like it, they can file suit in county court." They knew very well that the poor Black sharecroppers wouldn't do that in 1934 and 1935. That created a crisis, causing the cotton lobby to pressure Congressman Ed Smith of Arkansas, who headed the Agriculture Committee, to pressure the Department of Agriculture, which resulted in this small group of liberal lawyers being overruled and fired.

Francis Shea was ousted. He went on to join the Department of the Interior's Division of Territories and Island Possessions and was appointed general counsel of the Puerto Rico Reconstruction Administration (PRRA). Familiar with the quality of David's work and his strong passion for social justice, Shea asked him to serve as his assistant general counsel. Ernest Gruening and Carlos Chardon headed the PRRA, which had been formed to stabilize Puerto Rico's failing economy.

At twenty-five years old, David accepted the offer. He was enthralled by the idea of seeing Puerto Rico and other exotic parts of the Caribbean, having never traveled out of the country before.

The goal of the PRRA's $40,000,000 appropriation was to help the island's economy, which had virtually come to a standstill. Diseases and malnutrition were rampant, and workers' wages were low and woefully inadequate:

> The reconstruction program was intended to revive the sugar, tobacco and citrus fruit industries, which were the three basic cash crops of Puerto Rico, and to help with rural electrification. There is lots of water in the mountainous interior, and the idea was to harness it more effectively for electric power and housing. This was a tremendous problem in Puerto Rico because so many people lived in shanties, in some of the worst housing anywhere in the world. When we went there, we could see shacks constructed of cardboard and corrugated iron pieces from junk yards. So the mission was expanded and the idea was to build low-cost housing to replace the slums. This was the relief aspect of the program.

David and his associates lived in temporary wooden housing known as *los gallineros de PRRA* (chicken coops of the PRRA). These coop-sized barracks were constructed by the sea, close enough to manage a few lunch-hour walks and swims in the subtropical waters.

But during regular business hours, fifteen to twenty young men from the mainland buckled down and worked on various aspects of the program. It was a tremendous challenge for the young lawyers, who were often perceived by the native Puerto Ricans as intruders and interlopers.

Resentment grew as the number of mainland lawyers arriving in Puerto Rico increased, and there were complaints that the PRRA wasn't hiring graduates from local law schools. For his part, Shea followed the guidelines set down for him in Washington that required recruiting law review graduates from schools like Harvard, Yale, and Columbia. David, who had once drawn satirical cartoons for the Rutgers *Chanticleer*, paid close attention to the political illustrations in the San Juan newspapers:

> The paper ran a cartoon showing a ship unloading cargo. In those days, they used nets. They didn't have containerized cargo, but they would put everything in a huge net made of hemp rope. They would raise and lower it and then finally unload it on the dock. The cartoon showed this huge net, and in it were lawyers with their noses sticking out here and there. It was captioned *Abogados Importados—Imported Lawyers*.

As uncomfortable as it seemed with imported lawyers sticking their noses in Puerto Rico's business, the media criticism had no effect on the PRRA's overall mission. The US government continued its mandated hiring policies.

David lived in a PRRA chicken coop with his coworkers John Walstrom, a graduate of the Harvard School of Business Administration, and Rawlings Ragland, a graduate of the University of Kentucky Law School. David and "Rags" would later practice law together and remain lifelong friends.

But in the meantime, only five days after arriving in Puerto Rico, David saw the most beautiful young woman he had ever seen. As it turned out, she would change his life forever.

CHAPTER 6
Love at First Sight

Quiéreme mucho, dulce amor mío
Que amante siempre te adoraré
Yo con tus besos y tus caricias
Mis sufrimientos acallaré.
Cuando se quiere de veras
Como te quiero yo a ti
Es imposible mi cielo
Tan separados vivir.

Love me completely, my sweet beloved, forever deeply as I adore you. Your kisses and caresses ease my suffering and bring me peace. When one falls in love so truly as I have fallen in love with you, it is not possible, my angel, for us to live apart.

~ QUIEREME MUCHO (1915-1917,
MUSIC BY AUGUSTIN RODRIGUEZ; LYRICS BY GONZALO ROIG)
CARMEN'S FAVORITE LOVE SONG

David and his friends were enjoying a relaxing afternoon swim one weekend when into the club walked the most beautiful young woman he had ever seen:

I said, "Who is that?" One of the girls sitting with us said, "Oh, that's Carmen Matanzo. Don't you know her?" And I said, "No, but I'd like to," so she takes me over and introduces me to Carmen.

Carmen Matanzo gave David a coy, offhanded greeting. He introduced her to his friends John and Rags, and then she went inside to change into her bathing suit.

When she returned, David was enthralled; she seemed even more beautiful than before. He quickly learned that she taught physical education at a private school for young women, and that she was an expert swimmer and diver.

By this time, he was more determined than ever to get to know her:

> She was in the pool, and I swam over to her, but I couldn't swim very well in those days. I swallowed a couple of mouthfuls of water on the way, trying to get there fast. "This water doesn't taste good at all," I told her. And she said, "Well, you know, you're not supposed to drink it." I said, "I don't see any sign to that effect. Is there a prohibition against drinking the water?" She said, "Well, if everybody drank it, the level of the pool would go down." "Not necessarily," I said. "Fresh guy!" she responded. And she climbed out of the pool and left.

Undeterred, David continued his flirtation. He asked Carmen about her plans for the rest of the day, and she replied that she and her friend Martha were going for a dress fitting. Without missing a beat, David asked if he could go with them:

> She and Martha looked a little dubious, and then they finally said yes. We took the trolley, which was very slow in those days. It went all around the residential area of Condado. Fortunately, the trolley was going in the wrong direction. It had to make a complete loop and couldn't reverse, so if

you missed your stop, you'd have to go all the way around Condado again. And that's exactly what we did! It took another half an hour or so to get to her stop, so I had a good long chance to talk with her.

That night, David had a date with a young woman named Mercedes to go dancing at a Condado nightclub, but his gentlemanly nature prevented him from breaking the date. He phoned his friend John and asked if he would escort Carmen to the nightclub. "Certainly," John replied, "if she's as pretty as you say she is." David then phoned Carmen. His heart sank when she said she had promised to take her mother to the movies that night. Then, Carmen asked David to hold on. She cupped her hand over the phone, and after a muffled conversation in Spanish, she came back on the line. "I can take my mother to the movies another time. She said I can go," Carmen replied.

David described the nightclub as one of the most romantic spots in the world. It sounds like a scene from a movie:

> It was on the edge of the sea, fringed with palms and moonlight on the water. The ocean came right up to the sea wall, and there was a band playing Latin American music, slow boleros and rumbas. It was really beautiful and made for romance. We all went dancing. John and Carmen sat at the table next to us. I danced with Mercedes several times, and then with another girl at our table, but I kept looking at Carmen. She was a lovely vision. I went over and asked her, "May I have this dance?" And she said yes. Well, that was an experience! She was the best dancer I have ever danced with in my life. It was as though her feet never touched the floor. It was an incredible experience! I said, "My gosh, you

dance very well." And she said, "Thank you." She played it very coy. I took her back to her table and couldn't wait for the next dance to begin. I asked her to dance again. Finally, it got to be a joke because the people at her table would say, "Don't look now, but there's that man again!" That's the way it all started, and from that point on, the romance took off. I knew from that moment that this was the woman I was going to marry.

It took David a little more than two years and hundreds of love letters passing between them to officially propose to Carmen. Like many young men at twenty-six years of age, he admitted to being a bit skittish about marriage. From a practical standpoint, his work at the PRRA was a temporary post, and his career seemed still too uncertain to think of taking on a wife and eventual family. But he had found Carmen Matanzo, who was an extraordinary person in her own right.

Born Carmen Matanzo y Jaramillo, she was the third of six children of Dr. Francisco Matanzo y Gonzalez of Toledo, Spain, and Rafaela Jaramillo y Lago of Coruna, Galicia, Spain. Dr. Matanzo was a successful ophthalmologist educated in Santiago de Compostela and Barcelona. He pioneered a surgical process to correct strabismus (crossed eyes). He practiced in New York City and San Juan, Puerto Rico.

Carmen was educated in both Puerto Rico and New York City and held a cosmopolitan worldview. She enjoyed music, literature, and art, with a particular appreciation for contemporary styles. She graduated from the Savage School of Physical Education, now part of New York University, and earned a bachelor's degree in education from the University of San Juan. She taught physical education in Puerto Rico. Carmen was a natural athlete, track star, tennis player, swimmer, and magnificent dancer. She was well known for her leadership and coaching of the Puerto Rican athletes in the Central American and Caribbean Games in South America in 1934.

Carmen and David's love letters reveal a variety of shared interests as well as a deep romantic understanding and devotion to each other. They exchanged views on concerts, movies, art exhibitions and world news, and recommended books and magazines to each other. In the days before fax machines, emails, and cellphones, even communicating by ham radio had proven difficult, inconsistent, and frustrating. With the high expense of long-distance phone calls at the time, letters and occasional telegrams were the best way to bridge the miles.

Their descendants can be extremely grateful to have their beautifully handwritten letters as a cherished record of their romance.

In the spring of 1937, David left Puerto Rico and returned to the mainland to accept a new position in Washington. The evening he sailed home—Sunday, April 11, 1937—he wrote the following letter to Carmen:

> Dearest, I missed you the very moment you walked down the gangplank without me. It was the very first time in six months that we were separated, and I really felt it. I kept missing you more and more, and as though to compensate for your absence, you became the chief topic of conversation between me and everyone I met on board. You may not realize it, but you were something of a sensation.

Carmen wrote back the following day:

> Darling, although I am many miles away, my thoughts are with you, to greet and wish you a very happy homecoming. I

hope you find your friends and family well. Did I say before leaving you that I would miss you terribly? It's more than that, sweetness—I feel completely lost! It seems as if you have been gone for years—and it was only yesterday.

That summer, before beginning his new job, David traveled by steamship on a European vacation with his friend Dan Kasen, who had been one of his partners in the Newark law firm. Almost every day, he shared his adventures with Carmen, always sending letters that included his warmest regards to her mother, brother, sisters, and friends. Even as a carefree bachelor traveling through Europe, David expressed his unwavering love to Carmen in his letters.

Carmen responded with adventures of her own. She thoughtfully collected seashells as a gift for David's four-year-old nephew Freddie.

When David presented Freddie with Carmen's hand-decorated gift boxes of shells, the little boy was ecstatic. He sorted the shells, named each one, and pretended they were toy soldiers. David shared these details with Carmen, who was delighted to hear about it.

Meanwhile, David and Dan excitedly spun through Europe. Each had packed a tuxedo in their Gladstone bags and suitcases, trying to travel as lightly as possible while still displaying their best sartorial splendor. Their letters reveal a kaleidoscope of dazzling experiences as they attended plays, concerts, dances, and a variety of festivals in the countries they visited. David even drew cartoons of some of their escapades.

While in Paris, he purchased quality art prints by Cézanne, Renoir, and van Gogh. He could not have known then that these purchases would foreshadow a time twenty years later when he and Carmen would begin collecting originals by the same artists and eventually share them with the public.

That future, like all futures, was unknowable then.

As letters between David and Carmen flew back and forth, sometimes twice a day, their joys and disappointments were interlaced with terms of endearment. They shared views on timely events, such as the May 7, 1937, Hindenburg disaster. David had seen five different newsreels documenting the explosion, each one from a different perspective. He wrote that he found Fanny Brice very funny but that the Ziegfeld Follies was a bit disappointing. Carmen had read Margaret Mitchell's newly published novel *Gone with the Wind* and sent David her complete review of it. He saw a production of Shakespeare's *Richard III* starring Maurice Evans and told her it was inspiring. Their lively correspondence is filled with personal reviews of the movies they saw, plus the plays, ballets, concerts, and books they read. They were devastated when long-anticipated letters didn't arrive on time.

Carmen had been coy at the beginning of their romance, but now her perfumed letters arrived in a seductive penmanship written with green ink, and she openly expressed her longing for David.

In the volley of love letters between them, David revealed that his friends were so impressed with his description and photos of her that they could hardly wait to meet his Spanish beauty. Friends who had already met Carmen looked forward to seeing her again, and independently wrote her cordial letters. David enjoyed reporting on how popular she was among his friends, and Carmen modestly chided him for too often singing her praises.

When David felt ready to officially propose marriage to Carmen, he knew he needed to first ask for his father's blessing. Barnet valued his Ashkenazi Jewish heritage and its emphasis on the importance of family. David had to find the best way to tell his father that he planned to marry Carmen, who was of Spanish Catholic descent.

INSPIRING LEGACY

Barnet listened to his son's description of his beautiful Puerto Rican sweetheart and asked in Yiddish, *"A zay fil Yiddishe maidlach?"* which means "Aren't there enough Jewish girls?"

David explained that religion wasn't all that important to either of them. Carmen's late father had been a liberal Catholic and her mother, Rafaela, a theosophist who held a universal and spiritual view of God. David even suggested that there might have been Jews in Carmen's ancestry as far back as the Spanish Inquisition.

Meanwhile, back in Puerto Rico, Carmen did her own genealogical research. She visited relatives and close family friends in Caguas and San Juan to inquire about her ancestry. Her father had died in the early 1930s, leaving little information behind about his family, and her mother could only trace hers back a few generations. After some insightful questions, Carmen learned that her ancestors had roots in Seville, Castile, and Galicia, Spain.

By coincidence, there is also a Galicia in Central Eastern Europe, a region familiar to Ashkenazi Jews. That inspired David to tell Barnet that Carmen's mother was a *galitzianer*, a Yiddish word for a person with roots in Eastern Europe. He didn't say that Rafaela was actually a *gallega* with roots in Galicia, Spain. When Barnet met Rafaela at the wedding, he was puzzled as to why his *galitzianer* didn't speak one word of Yiddish!

Harvard Law School taught David how to build a strong case that covered every inch of legal ground. Now it was time for him to use his skills in a more delicate cause. He would write the most important letter of his life and present his official proposal of marriage to Señorita Carmen Matanzo.

As the saying goes, lawyers should only pose questions to which they already know the answers, but sometimes that assurance is only in the high percentage range. Still, David was quite confident as to Carmen's response.

In that spirit, he sat down on September 25, 1937, and penned a four-page love letter to Carmen seasoned with terms of endearment. He had received three marvelous letters from her that week and excitedly envisioned their future together in the modest apartment they would share after their marriage:

> I'm going to look around for a little apartment for us—bedroom, living room, kitchenette and bath. We'll just take it furnished for a few months, and then we'll both have the grand fun of looking about together for furniture, curtains, rugs, silver, etc., etc. I'd like to have a house in the suburbs near Washington with two bedrooms, sitting room, etc., so that we can have my dad or your mother spend a few weekends with us. I'd also like to shop with you for a piano, radio and Victrola. We'll have lots of music, if nothing else. I want you to know that everyone is very well here. I know you'll love them, and I'm positive they will love you.

They had talked about starting a family. Carmen had written:

> Imagine our children (every time I think of that, I get such a wonderful thrill, beloved!) They will have Sevillian, Castilian and Galician from my side and Russian and German from yours—whew! That's some concoction! Do you think we'll be able to handle them?

David offered some paternal thoughts as he continued his letter:

> Beloved, you thrilled me so with your question as to whether we should have a baby right away—the very thought of our having a baby is marvelous. I hope it looks like you! But I agree with you, my dearest, that we shouldn't be in too much of a hurry. We should have at least two years alone before we invite a third person to move in with us permanently.

He spoke of choosing a wedding date, regretting that he had used up his annual leave on his trip to Europe. He insisted that they would work it out, perhaps for late November or early December. The location was also a challenge—whether they would wed on the mainland or in Puerto Rico. As he closed his letter, he realized that he had not yet stated his "airtight" case. In the spirit of love, wit, and deliberation, he offered his formal summation:

> Darling, I have thought about us from all angles and have fully made up my mind, but look, I haven't ever put my question in the conventional way! Darling, I love you. Will you marry me? There! Now I can't back out (as though I'd want to!) But first, I must talk to my father and when I get his consent and blessing, I'll write your mother about it. After all, when her daughter loves and is loved, deeply and sincerely, can there be any doubt? But please say nothing for a short while. We can announce our engagement after I talk to my dad.

Carmen wrote back to David the same day. While the notion of a small, cozy apartment pleased her, she balked at his suggestion that she come to Washington to get married, not wanting to expose her mother to the cold January winter:

Can't you get annual leave advanced and come down, and then we'll go right back? I hope, sweetheart, that you will be able to do so. Just to think how wonderful it will be to live with you, enjoying everything together with you, makes me feel much joy and happiness. When it does come true, I know I'll feel as if it were a miracle and I'll be so deliciously happy. Beloved—yes—I'll marry you—but darling, I want you to ask me again when we see each other. I want your arms around me when you ask me, and tell me how you love me. Darling, it will be sublime. Just reading about it gives me such a thrill. Sweetheart, I love you with all my heart and soul. All my love and kisses and hugs and thoughts are yours. My darling, take good care of yourself. I adore you and want you near me very soon—always to be with you.

Overjoyed, David sat down to pen a response:

Now I know that it is all settled, and you shall be my wife very soon. Beloved mine, I am thrilled through and through at the prospect of having you as my own darling wife, my beloved. Sweetheart, start getting ready. I should have my car and I'll be able to call for you in New York in the style to which I'm going to accustom you.

Still, Carmen wanted the wedding to take place in Puerto Rico:

Your perfectly adorable letter thrilled me so! To read that I shall be your wife soon, that you want me soon, fills my heart with joy, and you shall be my darling husband. I am more than anxious to be with you. Dearest, can't you possibly arrange to come down for me? I would really like to be married down here. Please do come down and we'll go right back so you won't have to be out of the office for long. You could fly down, arrive here on Wednesday and then we could both go back on the Thursday boat. Do you think you could get a week off to come down? What do you think, dearest? Beloved, it will be marvelous being your wife and having you for a husband. I shall try to make our life together a constant honeymoon.

After much discussion, a diamond ring, a flurry of activity around the guest list, and a wedding gown designed by the bride herself, Carmen and David were married in Puerto Rico on January 12, 1938.

The newest adventure was just beginning.

CHAPTER 7

European Vacation 1937

> Broad, wholesome, charitable views of men and
> things cannot be acquired by vegetating in one
> little corner of the earth all of one's lifetime.
>
> ~ MARK TWAIN, AMERICAN AUTHOR

Colorful postcards in the archives of the Kreeger Museum display the vast array of sights and sounds David and his friend Dan experienced on their summer European vacation. It was a carefree, life-changing journey enjoyed shortly before professional job changes and David's marriage to Carmen.

As with any ocean voyage, the important first step was in the planning. David and Dan would sail on the Cunard White Star Line's RMS *Berengaria*, the pride of the fleet bound for Cherbourg, France, on July 3, 1937. Built in Germany, the ship took its maiden voyage only five weeks after the RMS *Titanic* collided with an iceberg and sank on the morning of April 15, 1912.

Because of that tragedy, crucial safety design changes were refitted into the luxurious *Berengaria*. Novelist F. Scott Fitzgerald used the ship as the setting for his 1922 novel *The Beautiful and Damned*. The *Berengaria* also navigated around the harsh restrictions of the Prohibition Era.

David and Dan were probably more concerned with their own travel plans than with the ship's history. They consulted their voyage-seasoned friends on what to bring. They planned their wardrobes according to the sartorial splendor of *Esquire*, the men's magazine fashion oracle. Wary of dragging too much heavy luggage across Europe, David wrote to Dan in June:

> The consensus among seasoned travelers seems to be that for our purposes, a tuxedo is definitely unnecessary. Eliminating it will mean saving considerable space since shoes, shirts and other accouterments can be left out. Moreover, my friends have continually stressed the importance of eliminating luggage. In short, since practically all of our time will be devoted to travel and sightseeing, and only a minimum to theaters, etc., there is no need for taking along an assortment of clothes suitable for a summer vacation at a resort. Two good suits, one heavy and one light, are really all we will need, plus a fairly complete assortment of sports clothes, slacks, etc. Please try to dispense with a trunk, if at all possible. I have definitely decided to take no more than I can get into a fairly good-sized suitcase, plus a Gladstone bag. Besides, I will have two rather large heavy cameras, both of which I will have to carry in my luggage.

Dan's reply came a day later:

> Although I agree that we must avoid taking anything but necessary luggage, I think that your regular tuxedo (not a summer one) and the accessories that go with it are such

necessities. Mr. Kohn insists that we take them, so please make arrangements to bring yours along. Equity requires that I carry one of your cameras in my luggage so you will have that much extra space for your evening clothes.

No doubt David was pleased about Dan carrying the second camera, but it seems that he wasn't totally convinced about the wardrobe. Dan produced an eloquent appeal:

I want to make one further effort at convincing you that we should each take that extra suit. Dr. Nash, his wife and two daughters are sailing on the same boat that we are. They are traveling first class. The doctor has advised me that he proposes to arrange that we have the "run" of the whole ship through all of the classes. Although I don't know the girls, I understand that they are quite nice. With formal attire, we could, if we wanted to, participate in the evening entertainment given for the upper stratum. It has been suggested by Mr. Kohn that you and I can pack our tuxedos and the accessories in one grip, and use them on the boat and in London, and then send it over to Cherbourg to be picked up by us on our way back. If, after considering the advantages you decide against it, I promise not to mention another word of it and to still remain your friend.

Dan's persuasion worked. The young men included black tie eveningwear in their luggage, shipped the grips to Cherbourg for the voyage home, and remained friends for a lifetime. Before he left, David wrote a letter to Carmen dated June 26 that included one of his cartoons illustrating the problems of moving lots of luggage around Europe:

I'll have two trunks, two large suitcases, one Gladstone and one large valise. In addition, I'll have a case of books, a set of golf clubs, a violin, a tennis racket and briefcase. Can you imagine me running for a train carrying the above enumerated baggage?

When they arrived in Europe, David continued to write to Carmen. One postcard originated from Geneva, Switzerland:

> July 14, 1937: This is one of the most beautiful places I have ever seen. The deep blue lake and the alabaster Mont Blanc in the distance surpass anything one could imagine. This evening, Dan and I ate dinner at a café overlooking the lake and we saw a gorgeous sunset behind the Alps. After dinner we walked along the promenade along the Lakefront—the whole town is very beautiful and very leisurely. Tomorrow we take an early boat for Montreaux and then a train to Zermatt.

On July 24, from Zermatt, David wrote:

> The ride from Viege to Zermatt by means of the funicular railroad was one of the most thrilling experiences I have had. The road ran steeply up the mountain, along the violently rushing Rhone, which at some points raced down from the snow-covered peaks with such turbulence and force that it created whirlpools and cascades that actually ran uphill. The river is milky white in color from its rapidity in running along rocky banks. Soon the awe-inspiring Monte Rosa and Matterhorn and Breithorn, all covered with snow, became visible.

The next day, David and Dan went mountain climbing in the Alps:

> We started at the base of one of the good-sized peaks near the Matterhorn about 6500 feet above sea level. We were roped together and during some of the ascent, the guide hauled us up the face of sheer precipices. What fun and what a thrill! You have to be as surefooted as a mountain goat. And guess what, darling? The guide said I was the best beginner he had ever seen in twenty years.

If Carmen was concerned about his safety, David gave her something to think about in his postcard dated August 1:

> We had lots of excitement an hour ago—an avalanche caused by the rain came down the mountainside about five minutes before we came to the spot, sweeping away the track. What a stampede and panic resulted! Several women fell and were injured. We're all OK and are on our way to Interlaken.

On August 8, David and Dan were in Austria:

> Salzburg—what a town! International high society dressed in Tyrolian peasant costumes wandering through the narrow, colorful streets. We heard Mozart's "Magic Flute" with Toscanini, Max Reinhardt's "Jederman," Bruno Walter's Mozart concert, a cathedral concert and Strauss' "Rosencavalier."

The young bachelors then spent nine days in Italy, where David considered signing their postcards *two gentlemen from Verona*. In Venice, they saw a "Tintoretto collection of 75 enormous, breathtaking canvases and a Venetian collection, probably Veronese." Five days later, on August 16 from Roma-Castel, David wrote:

> We walked ourselves absolutely ragged. Darling, there were of course the usual monuments, fountains, piazzas, buildings and parks, and the excellent art collection, but Rome was most interesting for its ancient ruins and its catacombs.

David wrote about his opinion of the city of Florence:

> It is one of the loveliest and most gracious cities we've visited. Besides the ancient castles, palaces, and fortresses, there are magnificent collections of paintings and statuary. The Uffizzi Gallery has the best Florentine Collection in the world, and there are also a number of Cellinis and Michelangelos.

From there, David and Dan visited France and won two dollars in the gambling casinos at Nice. They dined at an elegant spot on the French Riviera and watched water skiing. David described it as "an exciting sport—a motorboat pulls skis over the water at an extremely rapid rate—better than surfboarding."

David and Dan arrived back in New York on September 1 onboard the RMS *Aquitania*, a cruise ship notable for being one of the first after the *Titanic* disaster to carry enough lifeboats for its crew and passengers. In thirty-five years of service, the *Aquitania* sailed a total of 3,000,000 miles.

The European vacation was over. Dan returned to his position as a junior counselor-at-law with Bilder, Bilder & Kaufman in Newark. David was still with the PRRA, stationed this time in Washington. As time passed, their adventures became vivid memories. On September 3, David wrote to Dan:

> Let me extend my sympathies to you for the ordeal I am sure you are now undergoing; that of repeating *ad infinitum* and

ad nauseam the story of our magnificent trip. I have already gotten to the point where all that is necessary is mention of the word "Europe" and I start spouting forth words like a phonograph! I think it might be a good idea if we collaborate on a small pamphlet entitled "Our Two Months In Europe" and distribute this to questioners. However, it may be necessary to issue such a pamphlet in two versions: an unexpurgated one and a judiciously censored one.

No such whimsical pamphlets ever materialized, but David edited a home movie of the trip. He not only documented the journey, but his gregarious personality compelled him to share it with family and friends. Dan wrote:

Talking with other people who have been to Europe this year and other years, I am convinced that what we did, and the way in which we did it, made for a fuller and more complete vacation than I thought it possible to have. Leaving New York without knowing whether Tintoretto was a new color or the name of a town in Italy, I came back a self-admitted art critic, a member of the Kreegerian school of criticism. To show you how well you taught, I point out that on Saturday last I went to the Renoir exhibit at the Metropolitan and learned criticism of the paintings—what put the badge of authority on me was the trick of looking at the paintings through small openings of the clenched hands put up to the eyes. While there, we looked in at some of the rooms containing Roman sculpture, and there we saw casts of many of the famous originals we marveled at in Paris and Italy. The feeling of familiarity plus a bit of knowledge concerning the work, all produced a fine sensation.

INSPIRING LEGACY

In a letter to Dan, David noted that he had spliced together almost seven reels of film:

> And since each reel takes about twenty minutes for projection besides ten minutes for changing, rewinding, etc., you can see that there are in all fully three hours of movies. Some of the films are especially good, most of them are good and about ten percent are very bad, due exclusively to the fact that I moved the camera too quickly while panorama-ing. I gain some solace from the fact that I practically never missed having the proper light, aperture and distance focus. I bought myself an excellent projector and screen. I believe the motion pictures of Salzburg and the Rifflehorn are unquestionably the best. I have had two showings so far. We had a houseful of guests last weekend, so the movie show was well attended. Our roommate had a visitor, one Leonard Haber, a professor of art at William & Mary College, and a graduate of the Yale School of Fine Arts. Leonard, besides being a good artist and teacher, is a very humorous and likeable chap, and we have had several fascinating hours of discussion about the wealth of pictures and statues we saw in Europe. Incidentally, he has taught me a good deal about the history and appreciation of art. The reproductions of the paintings are probably the best buys we made in Europe, and I am genuinely sorry that I did not buy five pictures instead of three. I am glad that our visits to the galleries of Europe and the few pointers, which I was able to pass on painting and sculpture, have helped you to enjoy this very rich field. The discussions I have had with Leonard make me wish that I knew more about the subject and proves to me that you and I both would profit by further reading on this subject. I envy your visits to the Renoir exhibition. I certainly hope to be able to see that show also, one day soon.

One final letter to Dan offers a more "revealing" aspect of their trip:

> From time to time, particularly in Switzerland (during our bicycle ride around The Lake of Thun) and while we were waiting for our trains to Florence and in Nice, you will see rather surprising pictures suddenly flash on the screen. But under no circumstances should you evince surprise of your own; retain a certain stolid expression and explain that these were scenes taken at various nudist camps. At times you will be able to tell your audience that we were hidden behind some bushes; at other times you may invent your own story. At Nice, you may explain that these are pictures of how people change into bathing suits in public places, which is the truth as far as the Riviera is concerned.

The RMS *Berengaria* made its final passage from Southampton to Cherbourg to New York on February 23, 1938. The ship caught fire in New York (as it had on many occasions due to faulty wiring), and it took the crew several hours to extinguish the blaze. Determined unsafe for further cruises, the ship was dismantled in 1938.

Thankfully, David and Carmen's marriage, the voyage of a lifetime, came together beautifully as they sailed on with their wedding plans.

CHAPTER 8
A Portrait of Carmen

> In a dancer's body, we as audience must see ourselves–not the imitated behavior of everyday actions, not the phenomenon of nature, not exotic creatures from another planet–but something of the miracle that is a human being.
>
> ~ Martha Graham, dancer and choreographer

Long before David's European vacation, Carmen traveled with friends to Venezuela during the summer of 1936.

She was already a seasoned traveler, having lived in Spain while her father completed medical school. From 1927 until her graduation in 1930, Carmen lived in Manhattan and attended the Savage School for Physical Education, where she lettered in basketball and field hockey. After graduating from the University of Puerto Rico, she worked as a physical education teacher in the local schools. She also gave private lessons in swimming, diving, horseback riding, badminton, tennis, and archery. And she loved to dance!

Carmen was always an active, independent, and thoughtful young woman. She possessed a clarity and self-assurance that balanced well with her natural warmth and graciousness.

She wrote David from Caracas on August 27, describing the social whirl, just as he would do when he shared his European adventures with her:

> Once more, the social rounds began—teas, cocktails, dinners, dancing at La Suisse (the best cabaret here), made the rounds to the different, lively clubs, movies and tennis and swimming thrown in to break the monotony! Visited all the churches, famous for their relics, and all museums. Those Venezuelans are certainly true lovers of art. In my spare moments, I was driven around to take snapshots of whatever struck my fancy. I managed to get some very nice photos. Dancing started at 11 a.m. until 3 p.m. when dinner was served in the open air.

Despite the geographical distance between them, David and Carmen remained secure in their relationship. Their letters reveal no petty concerns that one or the other might meet an intriguing interloper who would drive a romantic wedge between them. Their correspondence displays a strong and abiding devotion to each other along with the delightful anticipation of sharing experiences when they reunited.

These experiences included learning the dance steps to the Bolero, the Rumba, the Big Apple, the Rueda, the Paul Jones, the Suzy Q, and Truckin'. These latter steps were part of the Lindy Hop, as popularized in the 1937 Marx Brothers film *A Day at the Races*, which Carmen and David had both enjoyed. As it turned out, whatever dance steps David didn't know, Carmen was more than happy to teach him.

On April 16, she wrote to him from her home in San Juan:

> For the past two days, I've been teaching folk dances at school, preparing for Mother's Day celebrations. The girls have taken to it like ducks to water, which makes it easier for me. You should see me! I danced with them right along until I noticed that some had stopped and were watching me—I had more fun! I love to teach dancing.

Carmen shared her friends' description of her insatiable enthusiasm for physical movement:

> My friends call me "perpetual motion," which is rather fitting and proper. I always want to be on the go, either playing tennis, hiking or horseback riding. We usually ride in the mornings, and in the afternoons after everyone has had a nap, we play tennis, ping pong and badminton. It really is a grand life, which I am enjoying to no end, and I wish you were here because I know you would enjoy it, too.

Recognized as an accomplished athlete and coach, Carmen was one of three physical education teachers chosen to chart the course for the Puerto Rican women's team and its future participation in the South American Olympics:

> May 7: This afternoon I attended a meeting to organize the program for the Puerto Rican girl's team that will go over to Panama next February for the South American Olympic Games. Two university physical education teachers and I have been selected to formulate the plan, which will be carried out in preparation for the selection of the women's team. It will be the first time for Puerto Rico to send such a team, so we have to be very careful that everything is just right because we want to establish precedents that will form a basis for future Olympic Games. We decided to follow the

> platform of the Women's Division of the National Amateur Athletic Foundation of America, or the N.A.A.F.A. Next week, the three of us shall meet again, put our program and plan of organization together and present it to the Olympic Games Committee on Friday afternoon. I shall let you know later how our plans went.

Carmen added that she and her colleagues decided that the women's team would only participate in volleyball, tennis, and swimming events, and that those wishing to compete could train and practice during July and August. Preliminaries were scheduled for early September, with semifinals at the beginning of October and the finals toward the end of the month.

In September, Carmen gave David her preview of coming attractions as they looked toward marriage:

> Honey, you shall have your teacher soon. We'll do a lot of swimming and tennis. I'll make an athlete of you yet! You can teach me bridge. And another thing—you are not going to forget your Spanish! We will also study that.

David had officially proposed by the end of the month. Wedding plans began in earnest, and Carmen good-naturedly chided him to stop encouraging his friends from joining them on their honeymoon:

> Darling, please think of me! Imagine my embarrassment, traveling under the close observation of four or five or more male attendants! Please announce that no one else may join the Kreeger's Consolidated Honeymoon Tour after October 18 (the date when you'll receive this letter). All

applicants after that will, if they want, form a Welcome and Reception Committee, and meet with us in New York or in Washington. The ceremony and reception will take place at Kiki's [Carmen's sister] and Ben's home. Sweetheart, I am so happy to know that you will be here by December 27th. I can't wait until your arrival!

On October 19, Carmen sent David specific details on the appropriate wedding attire for bridegrooms derived from the latest fashion magazines. The letter reflects the elegance of the time:

According to the Bride's Magazine guide to wedding dress for semi-formal, the groom should wear: Oxford jacket, striped trousers, stiff collar, white shirt, grey four-in-hand, black shoes and socks, black or grey felt hat, grey gloves and white boutonniere. Darling, let me know your choice of dress wear and I'll plan mine. Another thing is, please start making the list of relatives and friends in the States to whom you want to send invitations and a separate list of our friends here in Puerto Rico whom you wish to invite to the wedding ceremony, and those you wish to invite to the reception afterwards. I am making a list of all our friends, but I may leave someone out. We can check both lists to make sure we won't exclude anyone. And by the way, my dearest, my ring size is five.

Carmen was skillful at needlework and sewing. She made her own wedding dress after researching all the latest fabrics and styles. Confident in her own good taste, she also knew exactly what she wanted:

November 1: Please thank Anita and Marcia for their offer to help me in the selection of clothes but I think I can manage alright here. I have read a few Vogue magazines, which give all the information as to the latest styles, colors, and materials, etc., and most of them are available here. Anyway, I'd rather select my own clothes. I have already arranged with a buyer in New York for a dressy winter coat, evening wrap and sport coat. Other things such as hats, shoes, bags, etc., I can get here.

Excitement grew as the wedding day approached. Carmen had been hoping to marry in late November or December, but David had used up his vacation time in Europe, making that plan impossible. Carmen suggested that he bargain for additional leave from work, but David knew such bargaining was not an option.

And so Carmen waited. The letters continued:

Dearest, I'm pleased to hear that you have been practicing the violin and piano more often, and your description of the modern art exhibit sounds wonderful. I certainly would have enjoyed seeing all of those beautiful paintings, and we shall see many more exhibits next year. Jose Iturbi's program and encores sound grand! I heard him a few times before I came down to Puerto Rico and enjoyed his playing immensely. He certainly performs with such ease and naturalness, it takes one's breath away. Yes, my beloved, I do like modernistic furniture, if it is simple and not too extreme. It will be loads of fun to shop for our very own things for our future home.

As with all wedding plans, there was the inevitable discussion about the guest list. David expressed his feelings on the subject to Carmen:

Beloved, I don't like to argue about a small matter like invitations with my wife-to-be, but I honestly feel that certain of the office help would be slighted if not invited, whereas others won't, and that duties of friendship extend with equal force to office boys and cabinet members. Position in the economic or social scale is largely an accident of birth and luck, and our duties of courtesy, generosity and friendship should not be determined on that.

David and Carmen planned a civil wedding ceremony. While their different religious backgrounds could have been a stumbling block in their marriage, neither would condone that sort of intrusion. In fact, Carmen wrote about the unfortunate situation faced by two of their close friends who were deeply in love, although religious differences kept them apart:

> December 16: Adriana is feeling terrible about the religious obstacle that stands in the fulfillment of their love. Dearest, I think they are so foolish to let religion stand in the way of their happiness, or at least of their love for each other. Beloved, I am so glad you and I feel the same way about religion. It is really wonderful, the way we feel and think about so many things in life. It assures our future happiness.

Although no one in either family objected to their marriage, David's affection for his future mother-in-law, Rafaela, and Carmen's warmth toward her soon-to-be father-in-law, Barnet, would have countered any arguments.

As 1938 dawned and the day of the wedding drew nearer, Carmen wrote David about the Puerto Rican custom of "splashing in" the New Year:

> After the movies, we went to San Juan to Gil's home and waited for the New Year to arrive. We weren't there long before the clock struck twelve and we wished each other a Happy New Year. Millions of whistles and horns were blown

and plenty of buckets, pans and other vessels containing water were emptied over the balconies into the streets. That is an old Puerto Rican custom that is supposed to bring good luck. It was quite a wet sight and a hilarious one, to watch a few passersby ducking the water from balcony to balcony. Dearest, I thought of you a great deal and wished we could have been together. I'll be anxiously waiting at the pier to get the first glimpse of you since the last one on that unforgettable afternoon of April 1. All my love, your wife-to-be, Carmen.

On January 12, 1938, Carmen and David were married in San Juan. Rafaela and Barnet gave their blessings, as did David's brother, Morris; Carmen's sister, Kiki; and family and friends on both sides. The happy couple traveled to Washington and settled into their new apartment in Colonial Village in Arlington, Virginia. Ten years would pass before they would see Puerto Rico again. In the meantime, Dan Kasen wrote to David:

> Morris and Nat have given me glowing reports of your marital bliss, all of which makes me very happy. Is it true what they say about Carmen? Rumor has it that she has taken Washington by storm!

Thus, Carmen and David began the newest chapter of their lives together and sparked their enduring love affair in the nation's capital.

CHAPTER 9

Life Against the Backdrop of History

> The mere punishment of the defendant, or even thousands of others equally guilty, can never redress the terrible injuries which the Nazis visited on these unfortunate peoples. For them it is far more important that these incredible events be established by clear and public proof, so that no one can ever doubt that they were fact and not fable.
>
> ~ TELFORD TAYLOR, COUNSELOR FOR
> THE PROSECUTION AT THE NUREMBURG TRIALS

While David and Carmen celebrated their marriage, both were intensely aware of the increasing turbulence in the world. It was inevitable that tragic events roiling across the globe in the 1930s touched their lives. Although they were a safe distance away from the tragedies, they could not escape witnessing the rise of the Third Reich and its vast economic and military support of the rebellion in Spain.

As a man sensitive to human rights issues with a great respect for the rule of law, David was particularly outspoken against fascism's threat to humanity. He was wise enough to realize that global events do not occur in isolation. War threatens the lives of countless people who are innocently embroiled in the events, which are rarely of their making or within their control.

The United States Holocaust Memorial Museum describes the Spanish Civil War (1936–1939) as "a breeding ground for mass atrocities." The conflict began when nationalist factions of the former government, composed of conservatives, wealthy capitalists, and landowners, with the support of the Catholic Church, challenged the newly elected government of the Popular Front, made up of liberals, socialists, communists, anarchists, urban workers, and the peasants of Spain.

The former ruling elite rebelled against the new government to prevent communist control and a redistribution of wealth. The nationalist rebels, supported by the Nazis and Italian fascists, with aid from Moroccan troops, planned to return the country to its centuries-old status quo. Nazi planes rained bombs down on innocent civilians, and the outside intruders inflicted massive atrocities on the civilian population, indiscriminately killing thousands of innocent men, women, and children.

General Francisco Franco led the rebel faction. Joseph Stalin backed the Popular Front, also known as Republicans, who supported a communist takeover. The Spanish Civil War was extremely complex and horribly brutal as each side fought for authority and control. By its end, hundreds of thousands of Spaniards were killed or displaced. According to the United States Holocaust Memorial Museum, 200,000 civilians died by mass murder, mob violence, torture, and disease. The war caused 500,000 refugees from Spain to flee to France, where 15,000 people were sent to Nazi concentration camps.

---- INSPIRING LEGACY ----

The communists were defeated, but so were all hopes of democracy as Franco's dictatorship took root. The Popular Front continued long after the war ended. It would take two generations before democracy eventually returned to Spain.

Outraged by the cruelty, David wrote to Carmen from Washington on May 1, 1937, several months before their marriage.

> On Wednesday night we were to play bridge, but I saw in the newspaper an announcement of a movie that was being shown by the Friends of Spanish Democracy. It showed actual movies of the Spanish War, taken from the Loyalist lines. It showed very graphically the cruelty, the barbarity, and the violence in the bombardment by the Rebels of non-combatants in Madrid. Darling, you would never believe the horrors that human beings are capable of. The Rebels, knowing very well that most of the fighters were at the front, aligned with the Nazis. German bombers flew over Madrid dropping thousands of high explosives. Women and children and old men were maimed and killed and disfigured by the thousands. There were pictures of children blinded or killed by the shrapnel. What the Rebels hoped to gain by bombardment of the civilians is hard to say, unless they want to frighten the Loyalists by showing the terror, brutality, and horror the Fascists can be guilty of. Sweetheart, the pictures made us so mad we were all ready to take up arms against Franco and his supporters, but not against the Spaniard. There are only a few on the Rebel side who are really fighting because they want to—but against the foreign invaders of Spain who want to introduce Nazi cruelties and barbarities in a civilized country, for the benefit of a handful of wealthy landowners and millionaires. Sweetheart, it makes me boiling mad to see and think of

the damage and suffering the Fascist terrorists have wrought in the name of Spain and The Church. If people would understand that it is a war by the Spanish people—not against Spaniards—but against foreign aggression by Italy and Germany, I doubt whether there would be any Rebel sympathizers left.

Carmen replied from Puerto Rico two weeks later:

Before supper, some friends arrived to greet Mother. Among them was a staunch Rebel supporter. You would have been proud of your darling to see her stand up for the Loyals. I began arguing and everybody present all stood up (so it seemed) in one body against me, except Mr. Latore. He did not want to argue but would wink at me and make cheering motions at me—and finally stood up, shook hands with me and said, "She's right, you know." Of course, everyone thought he and I were crazy to argue for the Loyals. The argument came to a rapid end when Mrs. Latore and other ladies began to say goodbye to everyone.

David wrote to *Time* magazine's editorial department twice to protest its coverage of the war. An excerpt from his first letter is dated January 7:

Well may it be said, "the TIME is out of joint." Loyal militia representing a government duly and constitutionally elected by the majority of the Spanish people, and thousands of Spaniards voluntarily and enthusiastically flocking to the support of a government which they have lawfully created, take on a sinister aspect in your magazine, are contemptuously called "Radicals" "Reds," "Madrid mob"—terms obviously intended to carry a tinge of opprobrium. No hint is found in

> your pages that there are loyal forces striving to quell a desperate rebellion inspired by a handful of capitalists and backed by foreign Fascist powers, namely German and Italian legions sent to establish a Fascist dictatorship under the French border are favored by you with the grandiose appellation of "Whites," "Conservatives" with a tone of admiration and praise rising from every description of their deeds, their orderly, well-trained soldiers, even their bombardment and shelling of the helpless and defenseless non-combatant *Madrilenos* [citizens of Madrid], an activity presumed not deemed to be inconsistent with Franco's conservatism. The fact that Franco is admittedly seeking to establish a Fascist dictatorship in Spain, which every responsible publication except TIME is honest enough to make plain, is apparently considered of no greater importance by your editors than the fact that Franco is leading an army in rebellion against an existing government, something TIME seemingly does not care to discuss.

David wrote that he had tested his concern for bias by sharing *Time*'s articles with three open-minded and intelligent friends of his, all of whom were of Spanish Catholic descent and thus more inclined to support the Nationalist rebels.

> They had no hesitation in admitting that if they had no access to newspapers and other more impartial sources of news, they would suppose from your articles that a disorderly mob of bloodthirsty and wild-eyed Reds are ferociously but vainly striving to stem the righteous advance of a crusading, lawful force of conservatives. You may perhaps be interested in the fact that a number of your readers with whom I am acquainted have noticed the distortion and false emphasis which you are now employing in your news columns to point out your bias and have ceased to read TIME for this reason.

Time responded by mail on February 26, saying that it had considered publishing his letter and others like it but had not done so because "it has not been found possible to give space to these conflicting opinions." Clearly, David was not alone in his concerns about biased reporting. *Time*'s letter continued:

> Naturally, a criticism like yours is of great concern to our editors who, now as ever, have as their aim a straightforward, unbiased presentation of the news. We do not pretend, of course, that accusations of partisanship are any novelty, since every controversial situation brings forth charges from both sides. This is particularly true when it comes to such a highly charged situation as the Spanish Civil War, whose issues are so obscured by propaganda and misconceptions of all kinds. You make some points that it is impossible to pass off lightly, especially the testimony of your friends whose sympathies incline towards the Rebels. But it would be equally impossible for us to meet you on your own ground here. All we can do is take your word for it and offer our own experience in turn: that Rebel sympathizers have been accusing us of discriminating against their side, favoring the other. Accusations from both sides are no conclusive proof of impartiality, to be sure, but we feel it is evidence at least. But let me stress the more intrinsic points that TIME's attitude is genuinely impartial, and I say this with all deference to your opinion. Each week, we make every effort to provide readers with the most accurate, precise and objective reports possible without any attempt to assign blame or credit. Such terms as "Reds," "Radicals" and so on should not be considered swear words; we use "Reds" and "Whites" simply as convenient labels, giving some indication of the prevailing color of the contending forces at the moment. And TIME has made amply clear, we thought, Franco's Fascist attachments and

> the fact that the Madrid government was duly elected in February, however its composition may have changed since. We realize that if TIME's reports have not convinced you of our genuine impartiality, this statement of our policies could hardly be expected to. I am sorry that this should be so, and hope that you will at least keep an open mind as you continue to read TIME's week-by-week reports and let us know any specific points to which you take exception at any time.

David followed up with a second letter to *Time* magazine, dated May 18:

> For specific criticism of TIME's policy and of what I consider to be definite indications of partisanship and false coloring of news by TIME's editorial staff, I may refer you to my letter of January 7, 1937, to TIME, which I sent from Puerto Rico. That letter dealt with what in my opinion was definitely inaccurate and distorted reporting of the Spanish situation by TIME particularly in the omission from its columns of any mention of the fact that the so-called "Whites" (an appellation which is used by apparently no other periodical) are a rebel force composed principally of Moorish mercenaries, and German and Italian troops, engaged in carrying on a rebellion against a duly and constitutionally elected government of liberals, Socialists and some Communists (all of whom are misleadingly lumped by your periodical under the term "Reds." It is possible that I may have been mistaken in my allegations, but there has certainly been strong evidence to support them. I will, however, rescind the cancellation of my subscription, and try for a month to see whether I notice any change in TIME's policy, to conform to the fairness and impartiality so frequently boasted by that magazine.

David wrote to Carmen, praising her for her support of the loyalists:

> Darling, keep up the good work—rooting for the Loyalists—that means the people of Spain—the women and children and workers who make up three-quarters or perhaps five-sixths of Spain's people. The Rebels, who despite superior arms, equipment and money have failed to take Madrid or Bilbao, are finding out how desperately people can fight to preserve their freedom from fascist slavery, and to protect their homes and families against the brutal and barbarous vengeance, which has to become synonymous with Mussolini and Hitler. I doubt whether all Puerto Ricans who sympathize with Franco will continue to do so after they see the conditions he would inflict on Spain in two or three years of militaristic, aggressive and restrictive rule. Just as Germany and Italy have doomed any literary or intellectual or artistic growth in their countries, so Spain would also turn the academic clock back by a thousand years. So darling, by rooting for democracy and freedom in Spain, you are upholding a cause which is bound to be vindicated by time.

Observing that few people in Puerto Rico understood the serious dangers of fascism because the truth wasn't being fully reported to them, Carmen addressed the cause again in a letter to David dated June 21.

> I am glad to report that we have another ally in our ranks of Loyalists. I have promised to lend him the *Photo History* and *Nation* and *New Republic* you sent me. He has also noticed the biased information of TIME Magazine and I advised him to change to the *New Republic*. You know darling, the Rebel sympathizers here haven't realized the menace that Fascism is to civilization; and you know why, because they really don't read the truth about it, and base their beliefs on what they

read in the *El Mundo* and *Correspondencia*, which are terribly biased and print such sensational untruthful headlines just as a means to sell the paper. I am very glad and thankful to you that you opened my eyes to the real situation.

On June 23, David replied:

You made me very proud of my darling by spreading the truth about the situation in Spain. The bombing of Almeria and Guernica by the Germans was only a step in the continuous campaign of Germany to help Franco. But let the Catholics, who back Franco, learn a lesson from what Hitler is doing to the Catholics in Germany. Franco will do the same. Franco will have to kill 100,000 Spaniards before he can crush the Spanish people. I think that sooner or later, however, the real Spain will emerge from the Middle Ages.

On September 27, Carmen sent David an accurate and tragic observation of human nature that still rings true today, anywhere in the world:

As to our feelings towards the situation in Spain, remember that not everyone—in fact, very few people—have such high ideals of justice and democracy and consequently don't care about what Franco is doing as long as the capitalists and nobles of Spain may rule and profit by it without regard for the oppression and suffering of the Spanish people.

At that time, America's recovery from the Great Depression was still tenuous. The US government, along with a majority of its citizens, still supported isolationist policies that prevented any intervention in Spain. Few paid attention to Hitler's systemic reign of terror there, or in Europe.

As promised, David maintained the courage of his convictions. Confident that its reporting was indeed biased, he ended his subscription to *Time* magazine.

Ironically, just days before he and Carmen were married, *Time* named Adolf Hitler its "Man of the Year" in 1938.

The Washington Friends of Spanish Democracy sent David a fundraising letter that included the names of its officers and sponsors. It began with a terrifying cable signed by three famous writers:

JUNE 9, 1938

RECENT HEAVY FIGHTING IN LOYALIST SPAIN [stop] MANY AMBULANCES CAPTURED OR DESTROYED BY BOMBS [stop] MANY SPANIARDS AND AMERICAN VOLUNTEERS FIGHTING FOR IDEALS HELD DEAR— ALL OF US SEVERELY HANDICAPPED FOR WANT OF TRANSPORTATION TO CARRY WOUNDED FROM FRONT TO HOSPITALS BEHIND LINES [stop] IN HEROIC BACK-TO-WALL DEFENSE WHICH SPANISH REPUBLIC NOW MAKING IN HOPE OF SAVING SITUATION AND CHECKING FASCISTS [stop] ITS BRAVE TROOPS SHOULDN'T BE SUBJECTED TO ANY SUFFERING WHICH RELATIVELY SMALL SACRIFICE FROM US CAN AVOID [stop]

Signed

ERNEST HEMINGWAY
VINCENT SHEEHAN
LOUIS FISCHER

INSPIRING LEGACY

In response, a group of federal employees in Washington and New York organized the Federal Employees Ambulance Campaign Committee to raise money for the purchase of three ambulances. To facilitate the transference of funds, it cooperated with the North American Committee to Aid Spain, which had been authorized by the State Department to collect money for humanitarian purposes.

Fundraising correspondence from a group known as Friends of the Abraham Lincoln Brigade reached David in his new position as a lawyer with the Public Works Administration. The group was working to raise $150,000 to bring home 1,100 Americans wounded in Spain. Listed among its sponsors were actor James Cagney, poets Langston Hughes and Carl Sandburg, and writers Lillian Hellman, Archibald MacLeish, and Upton Sinclair. The group sought donations to charter a ship staffed by doctors and nurses to bring wounded Americans home from Spain.

It was to causes like these that David conscientiously contributed, always a supporter of the common man and his liberties. He made no secret of his anti-fascist views. His respect for the rule of law was born in his sense of fairness, which had been modeled by his father and reinforced by his professors at Harvard, who were some of the finest judicial minds in the country.

When David and his friend Dan traveled to Europe, they visited Austria but not Germany. Like many Americans, they had undoubtedly heard of Germany's outrageous laws against Jews and its aggressive, expansionist policies. Fortunately, the two young men returned home in September 1937, just seven months before the *Anschluss*, Hitler's annexation of Austria, on March 12, 1938.

To shed light on the historical perspective of the global events in David's life, Franklin D. Roosevelt was sworn in as president of the United States in 1933 in the midst of the Great Depression, only a few months after Adolf Hitler became the chancellor of Germany. Laws were enacted in Germany that permitted boycotts of Jewish businesses, forbade Jews from serving in the press, and excluded Jews from government employment. Under the Nuremberg Laws of 1935, German Jews lost their rights of citizenship and were prohibited from attending schools and universities.

Meanwhile, David and other young, ideal-driven professionals came to Washington, DC, to work in the New Deal and do their part in helping America emerge from the Great Depression, which had taken its toll on the American economy. The country's long-standing isolationism blocked humanitarian efforts overseas. One quarter of the population in the United States was unemployed. Many people faced starvation and the loss of their homes. Segregation and racism threatened the lives of Blacks who were subjected to the cruelty of Jim Crow laws. Mexican Americans and Mexican immigrants were forcibly deported from California. Family farms were destroyed by drought and dust storms, and when banks closed, individual and family savings were totally wiped out. Although Jews were not to blame for these events, anti-Jewish and anti-immigrant sentiments were rampant throughout America.

As far back as 1933, American newspapers reported on Hitler's atrocities as front-page news. Anti-Nazi protestors rallied across the country, with one hundred thousand people turning out at Madison Square Garden. There were boycotts of German goods and signed petitions calling for President Roosevelt to act. But Roosevelt insisted that American job creation and economic recovery were his priorities. Immigration quotas were strictly enforced to relieve "regular

Americans" of the fear that immigrants willing to work for lower wages would steal their jobs. As time passed, the outrage over Nazi oppression subsided, and newspapers turned their attention to national "bread-and-butter" issues.

On November 9, 1938, only eleven months after Carmen and David's wedding, Nazis rampaged through Jewish towns in Germany, shattering shop windows, destroying synagogues, setting fire to homes and businesses, and murdering hundreds of innocent Jews on *Kristallnacht*, The Night of Broken Glass.

The United States officially entered World War II after the Japanese bombed Pearl Harbor on December 7, 1941. While the United States never officially declared war on Germany, Germany became emboldened by Japan's tragically successful attack on Pearl Harbor and declared war on the United States. Patriotic fervor led young men to enlist in the armed forces. Women joined the WACS (Women's Army Corps) and WAVES (a branch of the US Naval Reserve known as Women Accepted for Voluntary Emergency Service). Civilians went to work in ammunition factories, building tanks, planes, and military jeeps. Scientists also joined the government to design medical equipment and improve hospital care.

At the time of the attack on Pearl Harbor, David was one month shy of his thirty-third birthday. He was married with a young child, and at the time had been misdiagnosed with a heart murmur that disqualified him from military service. Instead, he provided his service as a civilian in the Appellate Division of the US Solicitor General's office for the duration of the war.

Historian Clarence B. Carson wrote about the staunch idealism of the New Deal:

> At this moment in time from the early days of the New Deal, it is difficult to recapture, even in imagination, the heady enthusiasm among a goodly number of intellectuals for a government-planned economy. So far as can now be told, they believed that a bright new day was dawning, that national planning would result in an organically integrated economy in which everyone would joyfully work for the common good, and that American society would be freed at last from those antagonisms arising, as General Hugh Johnson put it, from "the murderous doctrine of savage and wolfish individualism, looking to dog-eat-dog and devil take the hindmost."

Americans were shocked when Roosevelt died suddenly of a hemorrhagic stroke on April 12, 1945, at the beginning of his fourth term. Less than a month later, Nazi Germany surrendered on May 8, 1945. Japanese military leaders and combat personnel refused to surrender and continued fighting fiercely in the Pacific. Two atomic bombs were dropped on Japan, first at Hiroshima on August 6 and then at Nagasaki on August 9, destroying military targets and instantly killing thousands of civilians, which brought an uneasy peace and an end to the war with Japan. On September 2, Japanese Emperor Hirohito agreed to an unconditional surrender.

In the context of global history, World War II was the deadliest military conflict to date. The systemic Nazi violence that fueled the Spanish Civil War ran concurrently with the violence in Europe before America's entry into World War II. Casualty records of the war indicate that nearly 80 million people died due to combat, disease, or famine. It is estimated that 50 million to 55 million civilians were killed throughout the world. Of the dead, 6 million were European Jews, whose culture had been virtually decimated, along with people of other religious or ethnic origins, various political opponents, homosexuals, severely handicapped people, and anyone who was considered racially or physically undesirable.

The Nuremberg Trials prosecuted nine officers from the Nazi Ministry of Justice and seven members of the People's and Special Courts, charging them with "judicial murder and other atrocities, which they committed by destroying law and justice in Germany, and then utilizing the emptied forms of legal process for the persecution, enslavement and extermination on a large scale."

David paid close attention to the proceedings. Telford Taylor, his friend and fellow graduate from Harvard Law School, served as counsel for the prosecution. Taylor spoke of fascism's deliberate suspension of the law while it perpetrated unlawful acts against innocent people:

> This case is unusual in that the defendants are charged with crimes committed in the name of the law. . . . But a court is far more than a courtroom. It is a process and a spirit. It is the house of law. This, the defendants know, or must have known, in time past. I doubt that they ever forgot. Indeed, the root of the accusation in this case is that these men, leaders of the German judicial system, consciously and deliberately suppressed the law, engaged in an unholy masquerade of tyranny but disguised as justice, and converted the German judicial systems to an engine of despotism, conquest, pillage, and slaughter.

David's sense of fairness and respect for the rule of law were etched into his character and enabled him to start his own law practice when his government service was complete.

CHAPTER 10
Cultural Changes in Washington, DC

> I pledge you, I pledge myself, to a new
> deal for the American people.
>
> ~ Franklin D. Roosevelt, President of the United States

In 1934, when David and other young professionals arrived in Washington to work in President Roosevelt's New Deal, they found a limited cultural arts scene. Government programs were soon formed that offered to help artists and musicians struggling to survive the Great Depression. Recognizing the importance of the arts in terms of their cultural benefits and economic recovery efforts, the New Deal gave birth to the Federal Art Project during the years 1935–1943. Sponsored by the Works Progress Administration, the Federal Art Project built over one hundred community centers around the country and supported more than ten thousand artists whose works were placed in nongovernment buildings. To this day, many of these works are still on display. The Federal Art Project funded and employed artists to create murals, paintings, sculptures, theater scenic design, and crafts.

By the time David and Carmen married in 1938 and settled into their first apartment in Virginia, the nation's capital was beginning to undergo significant cultural changes. David reflected on the times in his memoirs:

> The population was less than half a million, 75 percent White, 25 percent Black, thoroughly segregated in schools, restaurants, theaters, hotels, and housing. The neighboring counties had no more than 200,000 inhabitants, no less segregated. Trolleys were the principal means of transportation, running along Pennsylvania Avenue through several streets in Georgetown and up Connecticut and Wisconsin Avenues. The National Symphony, started only a few years earlier, consisted of about forty or fifty musicians whose livelihood depended on other jobs such as teaching, taxi driving, selling cars and clerking in shoe stores.

He described the racial segregation policies maintained by the major theaters in Washington:

> A curious dichotomy was presented by the National Theater, which admitted Blacks on stage but not in the audiences, and Constitution Hall, which had exactly the reverse policy. The latter precipitated a dramatic public confrontation in the late 1930s when the famous singer Marian Anderson was denied permission to perform at Constitution Hall. Eleanor Roosevelt invited her to sing at the White House. Three years later when she was again denied permission to appear at Constitution Hall in 1939, Secretary of the Interior Harold Ickes proudly presented Anderson in an open-air recital on the steps of the Lincoln Memorial before a crowd

of 75,000. After World War II, Actor's Equity picketed the National Theater to end its segregation policy. Rather than submit, the theater became a movie house, and for two years from 1948 to 1950, Washington theater fans had to travel to Baltimore, Philadelphia, or New York for their plays, but gradually Washington, DC came of age.

It can be said that the transformation of 1930s Washington into today's modern cultural metropolis began with the arrival of those passionately idealistic young men and women ("enthusiastic youngsters," as David called them) who had come to work in President Roosevelt's New Deal.

Years later, with the inauguration of President John F. Kennedy, First Lady Jacqueline Kennedy's sponsorship of the arts boosted Washington into the role of a world-class cultural center.

David and Carmen Kreeger took starring roles in that mission. As David's fortunes increased over the years, so did his philanthropy. In 1938, he and Carmen could only imagine helping to shape Washington into the grand cultural center it would become. As the years passed, they would strongly support the National Symphony Orchestra. David would eventually serve as the first president of its board, and when his friend, publisher Austin Kiplinger, followed him in that role, he referred to himself as John Adams to David's George Washington.

The Kreegers would also support the Washington Performing Arts Society, Arena Stage, WETA-TV, the Corcoran Gallery of Art, the Washington Opera, the John F. Kennedy Center for the Performing Arts, and many other art and music organizations, including many universities and colleges. Years later, they would host musical fundraisers and art exhibitions in the Great Hall of their home, an architectural masterpiece on Foxhall Road.

But in 1938, they were a young married couple, and that future had yet to happen.

In the 1930s, small-town Washington was just beginning to awaken from its slumber. In 1935, architect John Russell Pope was selected to design the Jefferson Memorial, which stands on the former site of the B&O Railroad Station where President James Garfield was assassinated in 1881.

In 1937, Pope also designed the National Archives and the National Gallery of Art. Construction on both buildings began in 1937, and both opened to the public in 1941. Unlike other capital cities around the globe, Washington never had a gallery dedicated to art exhibitions until former treasury secretary Andrew W. Mellon supported its construction. The National Gallery of Art became a magnificent structure that displayed masterpieces donated from Mellon's private collection. Other donors contributed, and the city began a cultural revolution that drew visitors from all over the world.

With visitors came increased traffic, and more parking was needed. The first parking meters were installed on city streets in November 1937, angering drivers who resented having to pay a nickel to park on a public street.

Meanwhile, Steinway & Sons celebrated the manufacture of its three hundred thousandth piano by presenting President Roosevelt with a 9-foot-long mahogany piano that rested on carved eagles layered in gold. Roosevelt accepted the gift on behalf of the American people and dedicated it to "the advancement of music in every city, town and hamlet in the country."

The Kreeger newlyweds bought their first Steinway piano to enjoy in their Colonial Village apartment. Both were accomplished amateur musicians.

Against the backdrop of 1938 was the panic ignited by Orson Welles and his Mercury Theater's pre-Halloween broadcast of H.G. Wells's *The War of the Worlds*. Thousands of Americans were mesmerized by the scripted radio bulletins, which reported with shocking clarity that space aliens from Mars were invading the town of Grover's Mill, New Jersey. It seems bizarre that the broadcast drove a nation into mass hysteria the night before Halloween, but it did. Frightened callers jammed telephone lines. Terrified citizens crammed into police stations. Later, when the panic subsided, the fledgling Federal Communications Commission developed rules prohibiting the broadcast of fiction that could cause panic and public harm if broadcast as an urgent bulletin.

David continued his career at the Public Works Administration as chief of its Legal Opinion Division. Then, in August 1939, he and Carmen joyfully welcomed their newborn daughter, Carol, into the family.

Soon afterward, David's friend and mentor Francis Shea was appointed assistant attorney general in charge of the Civil Division at the Department of Justice. He asked David to join him in this exhilarating opportunity:

> My work was varied, but principally I worked in appeals. I became Chief of the Supreme Court section that handled civil litigation and appeals to the various Circuit Courts. I had one district court case and two or three court of claims cases, but my work consisted of appellate matters in the Courts of Appeals and in the Supreme Court. I found it fascinating! I loved that work. I did not want to be a trial lawyer, but I was very good in appeals and was always well prepared. I had no nervousness in dealing with the courts.

INSPIRING LEGACY

Anything is possible in a court of law, and the Supreme Court is no exception. David recounted arguing his first case there:

> Chief Justice Stone stopped me in the course of my argument. I had said that the attorney general in the 1920s at the time had ruled one way, and that the courts had reversed his position. Chief Justice Stone said, "Mr. Kreeger, forgive the interruption, but I was the attorney general at that time." Of course, I had known that, since the attorney general had been identified in the case. "I remember quite the contrary," Chief Justice Stone continued. "I had ruled the opposite from the way you say I ruled, and the courts upheld me. They did not overrule me." Well, this was one of my early cases and I had worked like a dog on every aspect of it. I'd read every opinion once and sometimes twice; I had briefed them. I had my notes all arranged, and I had the case so beautifully analyzed that I remembered almost every detail. Nonetheless, I had the temerity to say to the Chief Justice of the United States, "I beg your pardon, but my recollection is directly contrary to yours. The courts reversed you." "I don't agree," he insisted, "but don't let me stop you. Continue with your argument." He asked his clerk for the volume containing the case while I went on with my argument. My heart sank, and I wondered, could I have been wrong on this? After a few minutes, Chief Justice Stone finished reading. He turned to me and said, "I want to interrupt you again, Mr. Kreeger, just to apologize. You were right and I was wrong." That was very heartening. He was a fine, fair man, Chief Justice Harlan Fiske Stone. I really enjoyed arguing before him.

David had another Supreme Court story about Justice Felix Frankfurter that took place in 1941:

> When I was Chief of the Supreme Court Section, I was very busy reviewing the work of others. We handled everything except the specialties. Taxation matters, lands division, criminal law and anti-trust cases didn't come to us, but everything else did. These included claims and injunction suits by and against the government and special regulatory litigation, appeals from the Court of Claims and so on. I had about fifteen or twenty lawyers in my section, and a good portion of my work was reviewing their work. When I decided to argue a particular case in the Supreme Court, I didn't have much time to read every single case that could be cited either for or against the issues I was going to argue. I didn't have time to do complete original research. I left it to a very bright young man in my office, and he gave me a beautifully well-thought-out memorandum citing all of the cases that I would have to meet head-on. I wrote the brief based on that memorandum, but I did not read the cases that he didn't cite because they were distinguishable or irrelevant. During my argument, Justice Frankfurter stopped me and asked, "You haven't cited the Floyd Acceptances in your brief." I said, "No, we did not." "Why not?" he asked. Grasping at what I was sure was the only reason it wasn't cited, I said, "Well, Your Honor, it's distinguishable from our case." He said, "Then kindly distinguish it." Now I recalled nothing about that case. I hadn't read it in years. The last time I had anything to do with it was ten years earlier in law school! I was really taking a flier! I knew that the man who had prepared this memorandum was a very good lawyer, and that if there had been any relevance to our case, pro or con, he would have cited it. I decided honesty was the best policy.

INSPIRING LEGACY

"Mr. Justice Frankfurter," I said, "I confess that I've forgotten the facts in that case, but if you would be so kind as to refresh my recollection, I think I could distinguish the case for you." The members of the Court covered their mouths to hide their smiles. Fortunately, Justice Frankfurter smiled too, and gave me the facts. I quickly recalled the case and proceeded to distinguish it as requested. Justice Frankfurter nodded. I believe he was satisfied, but what an ordeal!

David spent six years with the Department of Justice. Near the end of that time, he edited a three-volume work on the patent system and the right of the government to control patents on inventions that were designed by federal employees and financed with government funds. He concluded that the government must own patents whenever it sponsors, finances, or instigates the development of an invention or device made by an employee or a contractor. The inventor should receive a share of any royalties or a bonus, but the employee and the corporation should not have sole ownership of the patent. David also wrote two *Law Review* articles based on this study.

There were other tasks of great importance that required David's unique writing and editorial skills. Readers familiar with editorial notation know that the term *stet* means to ignore a correction and return to the use of the original words. In the following anecdote, David's editorial *chutzpah* struck again:

> One of my assignments was to draft a Federal Torts Claims bill in 1941 to end the traditional immunity of the federal government from damage suits for the negligence of its employees. I was also asked to draft a one-page message for President Roosevelt to accompany the bill when it was introduced in Congress. After familiarizing myself with FDR's style by reading dozens of his messages to Congress,

I prepared a draft summarizing the bill and the reasons for its enactment that I felt was completely in character. I was quite pleased when it was returned with only three changes interlined by FDR in his own handwriting. Two of them I agreed were an improvement on the original, but I disagreed with the third. I had the temerity to draw a line through that change and wrote "stet" alongside my original phrase that FDR had crossed out. It was promptly returned to me with my "stet" firmly crossed out and a larger "STET" in capital letters written alongside FDR's own words, which I had so presumptuously deleted. I learned then not to tinker with the presidential language.

By 1941, David and Carmen purchased their first single-family home on Norwood Street in Arlington. David shared the news with his father in a letter dated March 7. Its tone is warm, informative, and practical:

> Dear Pop, we are finally going to become homeowners. We signed a contract to buy a house in Virginia last Sunday for $10,500. It is an all-brick house containing living room, dining room and lavatory downstairs, three bedrooms and bath upstairs, a pine-paneled recreation room in the basement, and a beaver board finished room in the attic. In addition, it has all modern improvements, such as oil hot water heat, hardwood floors, furred walls (which means air spaced insulation), copper piping, slate roof and other features. The lot is very well landscaped and is surrounded in the back by a picket fence and a row of small pine trees acting as a hedge. It will be a grand playground for the children and their friends. The house is lovely, and I believe fully worth $10,500. We are planning to take possession on April 1st, and all of you will have to pay us a visit as soon as we get settled.

David's letter then shifts gears as he advises his father on the potential investment in an eight-family apartment building, presenting a convincing case for investing in Washington real estate:

> On the radio a week ago, a congressman made the statement that about 150,000 additional people are coming to Washington because of the defense program, and he called on the government to meet this problem by providing adequate space for the additional people. Already a committee of Congress is considering emergency legislation that would prevent rents from being increased too high because of the boom here. You know that I would like to see you invest in Washington property, first because I think it is a pretty good investment, and second because it would bring you here more frequently. Our new home will have a guest room (in addition to the baby's room), which is yours whenever you are in Washington, so you should be as comfortable with us as at home. However, I don't want to make up your mind for you because it is possible that you may have as good, if not better, investments in Highland Park. Still, I cannot help feeling that Washington is a good place for real estate, especially since most real estate agents say that at no time during the Depression did the values of property suffer to any great extent mainly because there were always lots of government workers present.

After the conclusion of World War II, David left government service, and in August 1946, opened a private law practice with Jesse Messetti, a friend from Harvard who had worked with him at the Public Works Administration. They remained partners for a year and a half until the end of 1947, when David opened a new law practice with his friends, "Rags" Ragland and Bernie Shapiro.

Of his time in government, David wrote:

> Since law school graduation, by far the most stimulating, exciting, and satisfying portion of my career was my government service during the New Deal. To be part of it in the years before World War II was a heady experience, an immersion in a tremendous tidal wave of legal and social change that left its indelible mark upon our country. I have found that my intimate involvement with this fascinating chapter in American history was educational and maturing beyond anything learned in college or law school.

CHAPTER 11
Karma and Reciprocity

> No act of kindness, no matter how small, is ever wasted.
>
> ~ Aesop, ancient storyteller, 620-564 BCE

After fifteen years with the federal government, David opened his law partnership in 1947 at a time when the United States was transitioning from war to a peacetime economy. Starting a new business in those days proved as challenging as it is today. The first few months were slow, and the phone rang only when one of the wives called to ask how things were going.

Years later, David recounted his good fortune at having met a remarkable man who had started out as a client and ended up changing the course of his life in a very significant way.

To grow his law firm's client list, David had contacted former colleagues at several firms in New York City to offer his services. One such firm sent him a case, but when he opened the files, he was shocked to see that he was being asked to undertake a collections case for a bank involving a $4,500 judgment. It was quite a departure from managing the Appellate Division of the Justice Department and occasionally arguing cases before the Supreme Court. He disliked the idea of being a debt collector:

> I phoned the friend who had recommended me and said, "I don't like being a collection lawyer. I sympathize with the debtors more than the creditors. I can't do it. I don't like to pursue people." And he said, "Look, take my advice. Take this case and maybe there'll be a better one down the road. I agree with you, collection work is not really an attractive form of legal work but take it anyway. You'll do a good job and maybe you'll get something more significant from them in the corporate world or in appellate practice." So I reluctantly agreed.

David negotiated more amicable and convenient settlement terms for his new client. As his law firm prospered, he handled many cases and enjoyed one-to-one personal contacts with those he represented. He felt gratified representing people like his client who had faced challenging situations. Perhaps he was influenced by the story of how his own father, as a relatively new immigrant to the United States, had been rescued from distress through the generous assistance of a lawyer.

From David's perspective, however, private practice was quite different from managing a staff of brilliant young lawyers and advising them on their appellate government briefs.

A year or so later, David's new client returned to his office to discuss the possibility of transferring the license of a mail order insurance company in Texas to the District of Columbia. It was not an easy process, but since new licenses were not being issued by the District of Columbia at the time, a transfer was the only option.

Since David liked to know something about his clients' backgrounds, he had learned earlier that the gentleman had been an executive in a

INSPIRING LEGACY

bond company whose family was originally from England. The client had moved to Canada and eventually became a US citizen. He had joined the Canadian army to fight the Nazis who had mercilessly bombed London during the 1940 Battle of Britain. The eight-month long reign of terror killed over 40,000 men, women, and children. David had been very moved by his client's story.

He met with the client and his associate from Texas several times, and it turned out that the associate controlled a 25 percent ownership share in the mail order insurance company. Not only did David facilitate the license transfer, but when he learned that the Texas associate was interested in buying out his partner, he also assisted in finding investors for the new company. Its business plan was to provide automobile insurance to returning soldiers and federal workers, including government employees. The fledgling company would be renamed the Government Employees Insurance Company.

Decades later, the former mail order insurance company would be known as GEICO.

While David had a clever and intuitive business sense, he admitted that he knew nothing about the insurance business at the time beyond being a policyholder himself. Nevertheless, he brought the prospective opportunity to the attention of several of his clients and colleagues. But for reasons as varied as the people themselves, none of them decided to invest in the new company.

David had become fascinated with it after reading several months of its financial reports. In November 1947, when he learned that syndication was an option for purchase, he gathered up his own savings and went to his father, who had set aside a modest family investment fund of his own. David spoke to his family, friends, and other business contacts, and each interested party began making significant commitments toward purchasing shares of the new company. The investment opportunity looked so promising that Ben Graham's prestigious investment group eventually decided to take a significant portion of the deal:

> We had to cut back our subscriptions so that this investment group could own 50% of the company. By that time, we had managed to reduce the price from $500 to $490 per share so the total amount for 75% of the stock was $1.1 million, the amount, we had to raise. The investment company admired the business plan so much it committed $700,000 to the deal.

In March 1948, Ben Graham became GEICO's first chairman of the board. David became a vice president and served as outside general counsel. He continued his private law practice and was invited to join the company's executive committee a few years later. Shortly after that, his former client, the bond executive, joined the company as assistant to the president, and David Kreeger soon became its inside general counsel. He would eventually become an executive vice president, then president of the company for a stint in 1964, and finally chairman of the board and chief executive officer from 1970 until his retirement in 1974.

Lorimer "Davy" Davidson, the bond executive client who had walked into David's office a year earlier needing legal help, joined forces with him and, together with Leo Goodwin, founder of the little mail order insurance company in Texas, established GEICO in Washington, DC.

David and Davy worked together for nearly thirty years. Davy became the company's president and chief executive officer in 1958, remaining in that position until his retirement in 1970. In David's words:

Davy was one of the best executives I've ever seen. He gave his whole life to the company. Because of his keen and dedicated management, he was ultimately responsible for its growth and huge financial success. Ben Graham and his group's investment in 1948 would later prove to be the single best financial venture its company ever made. This deal had been framed as the most successful closed-end investment company, and by 1973, the company, which we bought in 1948 for $1.4 million (for 100 percent) was worth over a billion dollars in the stock market, or an increase of about 700 times. *The Wall Street Journal*, *Fortune*, *Forbes*, and *Business Week* kept writing up the remarkable growth of the Government Employees Insurance Company and compared it with IBM, Xerox, and Polaroid during the 1960s. Within a ten-year representative period, our "little" insurance company beat them all.

Like the moral of an Aesop fable, David's good fortune began as an act of kindness towards his client, who later returned with an offer of a lucrative investment opportunity. The next step for David and Carmen would be launching the philanthropic endeavors that were an integral part of their love for music, theater, and the arts.

CHAPTER 12
Taking the Plunge into Art

> Mr. and Mrs. Kreeger will proceed with the same enthusiasm, the same energy, the same taste, the same determination, and the results will continue to delight them and their friends.
>
> ~ Henri Dorra, editor,
> "Paintings and Sculpture from the Collection of
> Mr. and Mrs. David Lloyd Kreeger,"
> Corcoran Gallery of Art, 1965

David loved to tell the story that when he and Carmen married in 1938, they filled the walls of their Colonial Village apartment with reproductions of great art. Prints by impressionist painters and old masters moved along with them into their first house on Norwood Street.

The late J. Carter Brown, director of the National Gallery of Art from 1969–1992, often spoke about the aesthetic importance of decorating a home with reproductions if one could not afford to buy original works. "It is heartening to see," he once remarked, "that this was precisely the way the Kreegers began."

INSPIRING LEGACY

When Carmen and David welcomed their second child, Peter, into the world in 1946, a larger home would soon become necessary, but not simply to accommodate their growing family. The Kreegers were just beginning to build their collection of original paintings and sculptures and had started to purchase a few works "here and there," as David said. They quickly observed that, like people, different artistic styles sometimes competed and required elements of balance and compatibility, too.

Early in 1949, David began looking for architectural plans to build a contemporary ranch-style home on a lot he had purchased on Fessenden Street in Washington. He contacted a California firm after studying *House Beautiful*. By 1950, he had hired a young architect named Walter D. Byrd, one of Frank Lloyd Wright's associates, to design the family's home. David and Carmen's working relationship with Byrd became a long-term friendship that included mutual enjoyment of jam sessions and sailing.

Construction on the home began in 1951. The *Washington Post* published an article about it on April 13, 1953:

> When a skeptical visitor to the David Lloyd Kreeger's new house said, "I don't know whether I'm in or out," she also didn't know that her words were the greatest compliment. That's just how the Kreegers and the architect wanted her to react.
>
> The California redwood and Stony Hurst ledge rock come right in from the exterior to the interior of the house. When the curtains are open, a visitor can look from the entry through to the rear terrace. Rock Creek Park seems so close that it could be part of the interior design.
>
> "We all like the out-of-doors," Mrs. Kreeger says. She has the house to prove it.

The article continues with a description of Byrd's reworking of a classic, centuries-old Japanese design, including the low-pitched roof, natural wood, and stone interiors. Carmen, a true nature lover, enjoyed the proximity to Rock Creek Park, where she and David often rode horses together. The couple generously opened their home for a modern house tour to benefit the scholarship fund at Sidwell Friends School.

After returning from a visit to Byrd's Florida home that had included a session or two of improvisational jazz, David wrote the architect a letter:

> I want you to know how much pleasure and satisfaction Carmen and I have been deriving from the beautiful home you designed for us in 1951. It has not only been a constant source of aesthetic satisfaction, but from the practical aspect has met our social, recreational, and day-to-day living needs most admirably, and of course for our two wonderful children.
>
> I don't remember whether I told you about the visits we had in 1952 and 1953 from several Italian and German architects, who had been sent by their representative governments to survey modern architectural trends in the United States. They inspected our home, photographed the exterior and interior from every angle, and sent reports back to their governments. They told us that they considered our home one of the most imaginative dwellings they had seen in Washington and particularly admired the relationship between the design of the structure and the terrain.

With the management team of David and Davy working together with other senior officials at GEICO, the company experienced dynamic growth from the late 1950s and through the 1960s. The company's success allowed the Kreegers to realize their dream of continuing their generosity through their art collection, which they shared with the Washington art community.

With the assistance of veteran masterpiece art collector Richard Feigen, Carmen and David continued expanding their nineteenth- and twentieth-century collection of contemporary and French impressionist art. As passionately devoted to each other as they were to collecting fine works of art, they decided to mutually approve their future acquisitions before adding to their private collection.

The 1960s also ushered in the marriages of their children. The Kreegers soon became grandparents and were overjoyed with the arrival of each grandchild.

Carmen and David were also delighted that GEICO's success allowed them to continue making charitable contributions to their favorite cultural organizations. Under the leadership of the great violinist Isaac Stern, they also supported the major renovations at Carnegie Hall in New York City. The Kreegers opened their home and hearts to benefit organizations they supported and remained steadfast in their devotion to the cultural arts in Washington.

By 1957, with his dedication and commitment to hard work in his role as vice president and general counsel at GEICO, David and Carmen were able to begin collecting original masterpieces by world-renowned artists, including the first of two Stradivarius violins—a work of art that "sings."

Antonio Stradivari (1644–1737) of Cremona, Italy, is believed to have crafted 1,116 instruments during his lifetime, of which 960 were violins. Only 650 of his instruments are known to survive to this day.

Modern musicians and scientists have long debated the reason for the unique quality of a Stradivarius. Some attribute it to the porous nature of the spruce trees used to craft the instruments, the trees having grown in freezing temperatures at the time the instruments were made. Others believe that Stradivari's use of a particular varnish is the reason his instruments produce such dulcet tones. Regardless of which theory is true, experts who have recorded and compared several Stradivarius violins recognize that each instrument has its own unique voice while all of them share a "family resemblance" in terms of depth of tone.

But even the best violin is woefully silent without a violinist. Although David Kreeger was a modest and self-effacing amateur, he had studied violin for many years and had performed before audiences, often interlacing his repertoire with entertaining stories. World-renowned virtuosi recognized him as an accomplished musician. David remarked that "just to have the privilege of playing music with them for ten or fifteen minutes is a lesson in itself."

David encouraged student musicians to play their chosen instruments for the sheer love and enjoyment of doing so. That, of course, is the true definition of the word "amateur"—a person who engages in an activity merely for the pleasure of it.

> Most people who study a musical instrument do not regard it as likely to give them their main vocation in adulthood. They usually go on to other things. But it is a real tragedy when they turn their back on music from discouragement and frustration.
>
> Music opens enormous new dimensions, an avenue to pleasure, to aesthetic satisfaction, to relaxation, to intellectual agility and discipline—because there is a certain amount of prowess just to follow the line of a Bach sonata. And you realize the greatness of the mind that put those notes together in that particular way. It is a shame to turn off any youngster, and the easiest way to turn him off is to equate the violin with drudgery and frustration.

> My message to high school students is not to despair if you cannot play those difficult pieces; don't despair if you do not sound as good as you think you *should* be. Instead, play something on your own level that you can enjoy. Keep it up and never turn your back on it.

David recalled how he and Carmen first "tested the waters" of art collecting:

> We were in London and it was 1959. Carmen and her girlfriend were walking along Bond Street, and in an art gallery they saw a little Renoir that Vivien Leigh had put up for sale. Later at lunch, Carmen told me about the Renoir.
>
> I thought the Renoir was much too expensive.
>
> Carmen asked, "Would we get more pleasure from shares of stock lying in the bank vault, or from the Renoir on our wall?"
>
> I recognized that she had a good point, and that was how we plunged into art collecting.

David and Carmen's exciting "plunge" had been inspired by their dear friends Earl and Irene Morse, collectors of Asian and Indian art since the late 1930s. Irene was the daughter of Adolph Levitt, founder of the Doughnut Corporation of America (DCA), who had made his fortune with the invention of the "Wonderful Almost Human Automatic Donut Machine."

Earl Morse was David's friend and a fellow graduate from Harvard Law School. When Earl and Irene married in 1937, they celebrated their elaborate honeymoon in Puerto Rico, skillfully planned by Carmen and

David. Earl became executive vice president at Adolph Levitt's lucrative DCA, enabling the young couple to indulge their passion for collecting.

Earl dashed off a letter to David referencing the "incurable disease" of art collecting when he learned that his friends' acquisitions were to be exhibited at the National Gallery of Art:

> I am very excited about your new acquisitions and am glad to see that the "disease" is incurable. Am happy that you were able to build up such a reserve of funds so that you could treat it properly. I am also very excited to hear of the National Gallery of Art Expositions; I only regret I was not aware of it sooner as it would have warranted a special trip. I will have to be more careful if my suggestions are going to be so lethal.

David responded on October 7:

> My new "disease" is so incurable that it is scheduled to flare up again at the Park-Bernet Auction sale on October 25th of the paintings in the Juviler Collection. Carmen and Perry Cott of the National Gallery will probably accompany me and perhaps you may also find it fun to witness what may prove to be rather spirited bidding. A Picasso of the rose period is included among the items to be auctioned and may bring close to a quarter million (but not from me!)

In December 1961, *Vogue* magazine reported on the Kreeger's newest acquisition of Vincent van Gogh's *Vase with Flowers,* including a full-page color image in the center of the magazine:

> The blue ravishment with white and crimson flowers, rich and intense but without violence of any kind, belongs to the Paris days of the great, but then unknown, Dutch painter van Gogh. Doubly exposed to both the impressionists and

to Japanese art, van Gogh put a little of both in this subtle painting, now owned by Mr. and Mrs. David Lloyd Kreeger.

David credited his appreciation of abstract art to his professor at Rutgers, Dr. Thomas Munro. When speaking before the public, he shared his personal insights from his perspective as a musician, informing and entertaining his listeners with new insights into understanding modern art:

> The trend in modern painting is to depart from figuration because one can get much pleasure simply from line and color. Anyone can read into an abstraction what he wants. It is an emotional experience, and it doesn't need to "mean" anything.
> What does a concerto or symphony "mean" in music? You simply enjoy the rhythm and the harmony of the work.
> In abstract art, the line is like rhythm; the color is like harmony.

David had also arranged for Carmen to sit for a portrait by Alfred Jonniaux. Born in Belgium, Jonniaux escaped the Nazis and arrived in the United States in 1940, becoming an American citizen ten years later. He was well established as a portrait artist by 1957 when the Kreegers met him in San Francisco. Jonniaux had painted portraits of European royalty and aristocracy, as well as a portrait of Franklin D. Roosevelt for the White House.

On October 12, Jonniaux shared his excitement with David about the commission: "[I am] thrilled at the thought that I will have the treat to paint her in her Spanish dress. Please bring with you the records of Spanish music which she likes."

Although scheduling Carmen's sittings in New York City often proved problematic, and several changes were made to the portrait before it was accepted, David was happy with its completion and wrote to Jonniaux that "it is attracting much favorable attention from our friends."

Carmen's portrait would soon grace the wall above the fireplace in their home on Fessenden Street.

In 1957, the Kreegers met abstract artist Leonardo Nierman while on vacation in Mexico City. They enthusiastically purchased two of his paintings, *Capricho* and *Ruinas*, and were eager to show his work to a wider audience in Washington.

David wrote a letter to Nierman that reflects his fascination and discernment about contemporary abstract art:

> The two paintings arrived in good shape and are now hanging in the places of honor in our living room. We would also like to be kept advised of your progress in the art world, and particularly any exhibitions in which you plan to enter your paintings.
>
> A friend of ours is the owner of a local art gallery and we expect to show her the pictures we bought from you in order to ascertain whether she would have any interest in staging a one-man show of your work. Her gallery has been quite successful from the sale of contemporary paintings, which she has imported from Italy and Spain, but none of them are, in our opinion, equal to your work. They are, for the most part, representational in the old-fashioned style, and if our friend can appreciate the stronger and more modern trend, she may very well be interested in your work.

David described the exhibition of Nierman's work held at his Fessenden Street home on May 6, 1959:

INSPIRING LEGACY

> We had an exhibition of the paintings on Saturday afternoon and about sixty-five guests came to see them. The Fates were kind and presented us with a beautiful sunny day, which made possible an outdoor showing on our terrace against a background of pink, white and red azalea bushes in full bloom. The general reaction was quite favorable, and five paintings were definitely spoken for, with an interest indicated in two additional works. The most popular painting was *Elementos*, in which four people expressed interest. All in all, we feel the exhibition went off quite well. After we have made arrangements for a showing at an art gallery, we will expect you to attend the opening.

David had purchased Nierman's *Arrabal*, intending to display it in his office at GEICO. However, on finding it too big, it was moved to the front window of the IFA Galleries in Washington. As it turned out, it was the ideal placement and a great way to publicize the upcoming October exhibition. David sent another letter to Nierman:

> We are more than delighted with the news that you will be coming to Washington in October, and we will of course expect you to stay with us. By that time, we hope our recent acquisitions of French paintings will have arrived so that we can get your reaction to them. We intend to write to the Director of the Gallerie de Rive Droite, from which we purchased a Man Ray, so that he may see your paintings.

On November 18, 1962, the *Washington Post* offered an article about Nierman's upcoming show:

> Nierman's second show in Washington will be held through December 1 at the IFA Galleries, 2623 Connecticut Ave. The IFA Galleries introduced Nierman to the United States

three years ago after David Lloyd Kreeger, one of the most discriminating local art collectors, came back from Mexico with praise for his work. If he has learned techniques from the old masters, Nierman's vision is his own as a painter of his time. He paints colliding asteroids, cosmic fire and the sensation of flight, more than "the glass or the banana" of classic still lifes.

David and Carmen had introduced new lines, color, rhythm, and harmony to art and music in the nation's capital.

Seven months before the Kreegers had plunged into the world of art collecting, a party was held at the Shoreham Hotel in honor of David's fiftieth birthday. After being toasted for his generosity and distinguished career, he announced that he was establishing a $2,500 fund for junior, senior, and vocational high school students in an annual slogan contest to promote safe driving among teenagers.

This was just the first of a variety of awards sponsored by Carmen and David. Many were offered to art and music students attending universities in the nation's capital.

Meanwhile, the art collection had outgrown the Fessenden Street home. Floor and wall space had become so scarce that the Kreegers rebuilt part of their home, expanding it to include three large walls for more dramatic exhibition space.

But as always, David Lloyd Kreeger had an even larger vision, and he was prepared to make it a reality.

CHAPTER 13

Upheaval, Recovery, and Survival

> Into each life some rain must fall.
>
> ~ HENRY WADSWORTH LONGFELLOW, POET AND EDUCATOR

Unforeseeable tragedies dramatically alter world history and have a stunning impact on personal lives. Like most Americans, the Kreegers were not immune to the tumultuous events of the 1960s.

America was stunned by the assassination of President John F. Kennedy on November 22, 1963, followed by the assassinations of Dr. Martin Luther King, Jr. and presidential candidate Robert F. Kennedy in the spring and summer of 1968. The Vietnam War escalated through the term of President Lyndon B. Johnson, and by 1968, Richard M. Nixon was elected president. The war raged on amid reports of casualties that were broadcast regularly on the evening news. Antiwar protests spilled onto the streets, and civil disobedience erupted in many cities. The shooting of four unarmed Kent State University students by the

Ohio National Guard in 1970 underscored the intensity of America's fear and division.

An economic recession began in the early 1970s. Nixon was re-elected in a landslide as new storm clouds formed on the political horizon.

Spiro T. Agnew, Nixon's vice president, resigned from office in 1973 to avoid prosecution for federal income tax evasion. The previous year, five political operatives working for Nixon's reelection campaign were caught burglarizing Democratic National Committee headquarters at the Watergate complex. Nixon was directly implicated in the scandal and its cover-up. Talk of his impeachment began.

In December 1973, Nixon appointed Senator Gerald R. Ford to replace Agnew as vice president. Eight months later, on August 8, 1974, Nixon resigned. Ford took the oath of office the same day, entering history as the only twentieth-century president who had also been a vice president, serving in both offices without ever having been elected by the American people.

Immediately, Ford granted Nixon a presidential pardon with the belief that it would heal the nation's wounds.

Against this backdrop of political and economic turmoil, "Davy" Davidson resigned from GEICO in 1970, having reached his sixty-fifth birthday. David Kreeger became the company's chief executive officer until his retirement in January 1974. As the US economy fell into a tailspin, GEICO continued under new management.

The economic downturn proved disastrous for the automobile insurance industry, which recorded some of the worst losses in history. As one of the smaller companies, GEICO suffered substantial and debilitating losses.

INSPIRING LEGACY

The company's stock dropped over 60 percent from sixty-five dollars per share over a two-year period, and the board of directors began a search for new management. After an article appeared on the front page of the *Wall Street Journal* in January 1975 reporting that GEICO was on the verge of bankruptcy, the company's stock tanked and settled at two dollars per share.

The insurance commissioner of Washington, DC began reviewing GEICO's financial strength and its insurance reserve fund. A possible option could have been the suspension of the company's operating license. The commissioner was reluctant to impose such a harsh option, which would have put the city's third-largest employer out of business and forced more than four thousand GEICO employees out of work during the devastating recession of 1975. Instead, the commissioner opted for a reinsurance plan. Twenty-seven companies came to GEICO's rescue, each recognizing that the free enterprise system would be better served by the company's recovery rather than its demise.

Despite the uncertainty of the company's future, Davidson, Kreeger, and the GEICO board of directors convinced John ("Jack") Byrne, an executive vice president at the Travelers Insurance Company, to accept the CEO position and embark on the daunting task of managing the turnaround and rebuilding of GEICO. And rebuild it he did, with the assistance of some fortuitous events.

After Byrne accepted the challenge, he assembled a management team that included renowned investment manager Lou Simpson as chief investment officer. Through Berkshire Hathaway, Warren Buffet purchased 8,000,000 shares of GEICO stock at two dollars per share. A longtime shareholder and admirer of GEICO's success, Buffet had great confidence in Byrne and his new management team. He believed that they would rebuild the company and return GEICO to its former successful status. Solomon Brothers agreed to underwrite a stock issuance of $76,000,000 of convertible preferred stock. And by the end of 1976, after stringent cost cutting and astute management, the company had approximately $137,000,000 in capital, which would prove to be more than enough to move forward.

During the period of GEICO's decline, David Kreeger did not sell any shares of his stock. He always believed that the company could recover and regain its previous financial strength. His characteristic optimism drove his belief that even in the darkest hour, there are always glimmers of hope.

Years later, Warren Buffet praised Jack Byrne for his rare ability to envision and strategize companies looking toward the future while also exercising the real-time daily discipline required to make businesses perform at full potential. Byrne was nicknamed "the Babe Ruth of the insurance industry" and received high praise for saving GEICO.

The company continued to grow and prosper throughout the 1980s. It weathered the recession of 1991 with steady management and value investing. In 1994, Berkshire Hathaway purchased all of GEICO's remaining shares and made the company a wholly owned subsidiary. Executives of both companies gave their assurances that GEICO's management would remain in place, and that its policyholders and eight thousand employees would notice no change.

Once again, David's characteristic optimism guided him through a very difficult time.

CHAPTER 14

Breaking Ground: The House That Dared to Be More Than a Home

> Congratulate yourself if you have done something strange and extravagant and broken the monotony of a decorous age.
>
> ~ RALPH WALDO EMERSON, POET AND PHILOSOPHER)

In the early 1960s at the Corcoran Gallery of Art, David and Carmen first met Philip Johnson at his lecture on the future of contemporary architectural design. Their art collection had overtaken their living space at the Fessenden Street house, and they were considering building a new home.

Already in tune with contemporary architecture and its embrace of the natural environment, the Kreegers met with Johnson and his associate Richard Foster to discuss the project. They attended numerous planning sessions before the dream of a new home became a reality.

At first, Johnson refused the job, but he soon reconsidered upon learning that David and Carmen were kindred spirits in his own passion of art collecting. *Time* magazine summarized their first meeting in a simple anecdote that exaggerated Johnson's immediate acceptance:

> "Too bad," said Kreeger when Johnson first turned him down. "We had hoped you would help us with a dilemma."
> "What's that?" asked Johnson, perking up.
> "We like lots of glass, but we need wall space for our collection."
> "Interesting," said Johnson. "I can think of nothing better than to live in a museum, as long as it's homey."

David purchased the 5½-acre lot on Foxhall Road in August 1963 from the Trust of Olga R. Graves, a cousin of Theodore Roosevelt. The large two-story house with a slate roof and leaded glass casement windows was demolished to make way for Johnson's neo-Mediterranean domed design.

Johnson began his initial plans. He submitted a watercolor rendering of the home's exterior and presented his clients with his proposed model. Upon further discussion, the Kreegers approved the final design. In March 1965, they broke ground to begin building.

During the home's planning and construction, a great deal of speculation stirred among neighbors and those who traveled down Foxhall Road. Gwen Dobson of the *Evening Star* described it this way:

> The curiosity is understandable because the aura of the structure is indeed ambivalent. Is it a museum to be lived in now, or a home that will eventually become a museum?

David Kreeger and Philip Johnson were two distinctly different personalities socially and politically, and yet they bonded around their mutual appreciation of art and the shared belief that architecture is experienced through the sensation of physical movement. Johnson's philosophy of procession—experiencing the space one moved through and how it felt entering the next one—expresses the comfort a visitor feels while moving from one gallery to another through a vast space. This ease of movement while viewing and reflecting on the art on display is easily experienced in the Kreeger Museum. Obviously, that feeling also appealed to David and Carmen.

The following vignette from an article written by Cleveland Amory for the May 1964 issue of *Vogue* magazine offers a unique portrayal of Johnson:

> Philip Johnson is that rarity, an architect who designs his buildings like a sculpture, who uses sculpture as part of his buildings, who starts off each venture—art gallery, house, theater, synagogue, church, office building—with a soaring theorem, its principles not new, but its conclusions daring. . . . He is a quick minded, clipped talker, a dasher rather than a contemplative when the work is rushing along. An architect who does some of his most courageous efforts for private clients, he prefers to work with scale models. That house, deliberately built for a great art collection, has three main characteristics: it is of travertine, it has cross-vaulted domes, and it has the proper vistas.

Frank Getlein of the *Washington Sunday Evening Star* wrote about Johnson's design and how it met the Kreeger's specific needs:

> The architectural problem the Kreegers posed to Johnson was a home with lots of walls for hanging pictures and at the same time lots of openness to nature.
> The problem is magnificently solved. Every room on the main floor has one glass wall, and there is plenty of wall for pictures. There are more Monets in the collection than

paintings by any other artist, and eight of them are hung in the dining room.

There's the link. The spirit of the Impressionists brought art and nature together in a quite different way from any earlier joining of that familiar pair. Their love of nature shining and sparkling and always at hand animates the openness of the Kreeger house.

Carmen's love of nature is apparent with the inclusion of an atrium garden inside the house. Louise Odiorne, an innovative landscape architect and inventor, was commissioned to design it. In a June 18, 1967, *Washington Post* article about the garden, writer Wolf von Eckhardt described Odiorne as a cross between Buckminster Fuller, Frederick Law Olmstead, Luther Burbank, and Simone de Beauvoir.

In many ways, she was ahead of her time:

> Along with her structural inventions, Mrs. Odiorne, who was trained at Harvard and MIT, has done extensive research and experimentation in the kind of plants that do best in her "man-nature environment"—plants, she says, "that thrive within human comfort tolerance ranges." She is particularly interested in plants that are productive, that flower and bear fruit or whose leaves are edible.
>
> Mrs. Odiorne believes that her application of technology to indoor gardening, and that the new ways of living with plants which this brings, can vastly improve the man-made environment.
>
> "It is time that women became interested in technology and design and started to explore all their potentials for creating a better environment."

INSPIRING LEGACY

Because of her fascination with Johnson's own glass home in New Canaan, Connecticut, Odiorne received her first commission when she called on him personally. When Johnson described the atrium garden he was planning for the Kreeger home, Odiorne asked what plants he was considering for the space. Johnson replied that such knowledge wasn't his specialty, and after a long pause, added that he knew no such expert in that field.

It seems to have quickly dawned on him that he was standing in the presence of one, because he immediately commissioned Odiorne to work on the garden in the Kreeger home. Unfortunately, the atrium had already been built, and so it was somewhat late for her to integrate well-suited plants for the enclosed space and to environmentally coordinate them into the rest of the house. Still, Odiorne referred to the atrium in the Kreeger home "as a garden to look at, but not to live in."

About the atrium, reporter Wolf von Eckhardt wrote:

> The Kreeger's interior garden is nevertheless a verdant gem that will do full justice to what promises to be one of the most beautiful homes in this century.

Carmen's atrium garden was featured in a 1968 article in the *Washington Post*. It demonstrates her love for and attention to the exotic space. But as with any collection of living plants, the garden has changed with the passage of time. Here is a glimpse of the original atrium:

> A lush tropical garden, bright with blossoms of bougainvillea, oleander and anthurium, is a surprise in the midst of the disciplined glass and marble of the monumental new house of Mr. and Mrs. David Lloyd Kreeger. The glass-enclosed, domed garden atrium not only pleases the eye, but represents for Mrs. Kreeger a link with her childhood in Puerto

Rico, something she has dreamed for years of having in not-quite-tropical Washington.

Architect Johnson and Carmen Kreeger each made concessions in the process of keeping the aspects of gallery and home in balance. The tropical garden, with a soil bed that extends ten feet down through the foundation of the house into the earth, is one of these personal touches.

Carmen's artistic and well-integrated approach to decorating was described in a Sunday *Washington Post Magazine* article by Helen Hendry. Interior designer Samuel Morrow gave details of the eighteenth-century furnishings and French antiques in shades of peach, apricot, and blue. These colors lent warmth to the Kreeger home in 1968. However, since its 1994 rebirth as a museum, the couple's furnishings are gone, and only Morrow's words remain to spark the imagination:

> Furniture in the central part is relatively sparse so that each painting and piece of sculpture may be enjoyed in luxurious space. Savonnerie carpets in the Great Hall are in a tapestry-like design of colors taken from the paintings. "And the Chinese carpet in the dining room," said Mr. Morrow, "just happened to have colors with Monet tones." It also sets off the Regency banquet table and large Hepplewhite sideboard beneath Monet's *Water Lilies*. In the stair hall, the red accent of Miró and Kandinsky paintings is repeated on a pair of velvet banquette cushions and in the carpeting of the welded bronze filigree staircase.

Ever protective of their privacy, Carmen refused to allow any paintings or sculptures in the master bedroom because she knew all too well that David would usher people in like a docent to see the artwork at any time, very enthusiastically and quite unannounced.

"Living with great art," Mr. Kreeger said, "is very satisfying, not so much being able to see the pictures so frequently as it is to share them with our friends and our guests who enjoy them with us."

While Carmen shared David's enthusiasm, her "no artwork in the master bedroom" rule prevailed.

In December 1967, the *Washington Post*'s Maxine Cheshire reported on Philip Johnson's disappointment regarding the use of antique furnishings in his neo-Mediterranean designed home:

> Johnson wanted starkly modern black leather and shiny chrome furniture used in his architectural masterpiece. He even designed some chairs and sofas for the rooms himself.
>
> But these were rejected by the owners as not being elegant or grand enough in scale for a residence that has been hailed as the finest to be built in Washington for a century.
>
> The interior designer, Washington's Sam Morrow, agreed with the Kreegers that the austere furnishings suggested by Johnson were too reminiscent of Dulles Airport. "With a Great Hall 60 feet long and with ceilings 25 feet high," says Morrow, "it would have looked like a very elegant airport waiting room."

At least Johnson and Morrow agreed on the fabric and texture of the wall coverings, which served a special purpose:

> The walls are covered with beige cotton carpeting so that the Kreeger's valuable collection of paintings can be moved around without nail holes showing. Windows are hung with a tussah silk in the same neutral shade, chosen to blend with

the travertine marble. All this soothing background simplicity is some consolation to Johnson, but he is still "very sad."

"I haven't lost my affection for the Kreegers," he says, "but this is definitely the last private house I will ever do."

Johnson eventually reconsidered and went on to design more private homes.

In the 1960s, it was customary for an American house to have a recreation room downstairs, but the Kreeger home was not typical of its time. The downstairs had been divided into three separate galleries for use as exhibition and entertainment space. The *New York Times* carried a story about this feature under the headline "The Great Hall: A Mansion Is Attached":

> Downstairs, large vivid 20th century art—some of it pop—fills Gallery C [now known as the Contemporary Gallery] and there are sofas and chairs left over from the Kreeger's previous home in Washington, but no rugs. "We wanted the feel of a gallery," Mr. Kreeger said. The French impressionists live upstairs quite in harmony with the French antiques.

With the able assistance of renowned art collector Warren Robbins, the Kreegers' growing collection of African masks and carvings were originally displayed throughout the house. In 1964, Robbins had been the principal founder of the Museum of African Art, located inside what had been the home of abolitionist and statesman Frederick Douglass. Robbins's museum merged with the Smithsonian Institution in 1979, forming what is now the National Museum of African Art. David and Carmen became its ardent supporters.

Robbins wrote the following to Carmen on May 16, 1966:

> With your recent acquisitions of African sculpture to be displayed among the post-impressionist works in your own collection, you and Dave are the first ones in Washington to begin to give due recognition of the role which African art has played in the development of modern western art. This is a realm, therefore, in which art can come to play a vital role in promoting mutual respect, dignity, and understanding between two segments of our population, and the role which you can play as a pioneer in this educational direction can be an extremely important one.

While the Kreeger home was under construction, its unique design and ultimate purpose made it impossible to escape media attention. From 1964 through 1969, twenty-seven major newspapers and magazines across the country wrote about the house, including the *San Francisco Chronicle*, *House Beautiful*, and the *Chicago Tribune*.

Less than six months after the Kreegers had moved in, media requests to tour the home were interfering with the couple's privacy. As David explained to a reporter from the *Baltimore Sun*:

> Requests came from so many groups and organizations—philanthropic, social, cultural, educational. The tours in the spring and fall are allowed for about 300 people so that we can accommodate five or six organizations. . . . After all, it is a private home. If we had a waiting list, it would stretch out to fifteen years.

David's good friend Earl Morse suggested that the Kreegers invite media representatives for a "once and for all gathering" to manage the somewhat frenetic demand. The date chosen was May 8, 1968, with the condition that no articles would be published before May 19. Reporters and photographers would have the opportunity to speak with the Kreegers, Johnson, and Morrow, and they would be provided with a press kit that answered frequently asked questions about the house, its furnishings, the art collections, and all topics except cost, which was to remain a private matter.

But the spring and summer of 1968 were times of upheaval in America, jolted by antiwar protests and the assassinations of Dr. Martin Luther King, Jr., and Robert F. Kennedy. David believed that a story about his house would be inappropriate in the wake of such tragedies, and so the press tour was postponed. Eventually, it was held in September.

In 1994, four years after David's passing, Philip Johnson's associate, Richard Foster, offered his own detailed recollections of the construction in response to questions from Adele Platt, a student at Mount Vernon College for Women:

> From the beginning, the Kreeger house was to serve a double function. First, it was to be the Kreeger's home, and second, to house their fabulous art collection. It required a detailed study of the concepts of living, and answers to those concepts. For example, they loved music, and there had to be a place where they could hold musicales. The challenge was to design a home with intimate family spaces, public spaces, outdoor spaces for lounging and viewing sculpture, where climate, acoustics and light control were essential elements to be considered. Above all, the art was to be shown to advantage in every corner of the house. Such a design doesn't

happen overnight—it takes time to digest all these elements and to finally work out a solution that seems inevitable. . .

As I recall, the sources of inspiration for the domed roof/ceil form can be found in the projects we were doing at the same time. They all had an historic connotation. For example, the Pre-Columbian Gold Museum at Dumbarton Oaks with its domes; the Munson-William Proctor Museum with its façade of arches; the Amon Carter Museum with arches and prostyle portico; the room in Philip's own guest house; and the pavilion design in his lower field. All these designs were a play on classical forms. The influence of the historic work of Palladio can be considered, but in the final analysis, it is a synthesis of many historic examples that, when amalgamated into one design, answers a specific problem. The fact that the house is right for the site, and satisfied the complex client challenges, is a measure of its worth. . .

The 25-foot height of the Great Room is not atypical of the homes we were creating at the time. For example, the living rooms of both the Boissonnas and Wiley houses were of great height. The increase in room volume does help in solving (not all) acoustical problems. I believe height, correctly proportioned, adds to the nobility of a room. The trick is to create spaces comprised of low ceilings and tight walls to prepare those passing into the Great Room for the surprise of the "expanded" space. The Egyptians knew this principle and used it in their temple designs. It becomes a special experience that is recalled when other details fade from memory.

Carmen asked Johnson to include an elaborate staircase similar to the one at Lincoln Center in New York City. Two years earlier, artist Edward Meshekoff had designed the three-tier bronze filigree for its foyer. Fabricated by a team of eight craftsmen, the Kreeger Museum's railing was constructed by pouring molten bronze over steel rods attached to frames. It consists of twenty panels—six rectangles and fourteen parallelograms—and no two sections are alike.

Meshekoff's work can also be seen in large office buildings in New York and Albany. A prolific artist who crafted mosaics, stained glass, and murals for buildings in Puerto Rico, he also illustrated children's books.

Richard Foster concluded his remarks with the following sentiment:

> The only other information on the house that I would share is that Carmen and David Kreeger were two of the most intelligent, sympathetic, and in their way, daring clients, that I have known. I wish there were many more like them. What an interesting world we would share!

Philip Johnson designed an intriguing and innovative space that has been highly praised over the years by historians and critics of architecture. Its intended functions—first as a home and later as a museum—have served with grandeur. To this day, concerts in the Great Hall presenting a variety of musical styles resonate brilliantly with the sparkling acoustics of the museum's cross-vaulted domes.

CHAPTER 15

Shakespeare On Trial: The Moot Court

> All your writers do consent that ipse* is he.
> Now, you are not ipse, for I am he.
>
> – Shakespeare's "As You Like It" Act V, Scene I
> (*ipse is Latin for "actually" and "himself")

David Kreeger was not the first (nor would he be the last) to have doubts about the Shakespeare authorship.

President John Adams questioned it, too.

"There is nothing preserved of this great genius [Shakespeare] which might inform us what education, what company, what accident turned his mind to letters and drama," Adams wrote.

Mark Twain argued in "Is Shakespeare Dead?" that all biographies about the man from Stratford were built on conjecture. The supposed grain merchant-turned-playwright never had studied law, and yet the Shakespeare plays are replete with a high level of legal expertise. Besides, no one in Stratford had ever recognized their neighbor as a playwright, even at his death.

Sigmund Freud believed that "[t]he man from Stratford has nothing at all to justify his claim, whereas [the seventeenth earl of] Oxford has almost everything."

Actor Jeremy Irons has said, "There is room for reasonable doubt about the identity of William Shakespeare, and it is an important question for anyone seeking to understand the works, the formative literary culture in which they were produced, or the nature of literary creativity and genius."

During his career, David had argued numerous cases before the Supreme Court that led him to form close friendships with those who sat on the bench of the highest court in the land. In 1987, he asked Justices Brennan, Blackman, and Stevens to preside over a moot court on the Shakespeare authorship to call the public's attention to the seventeenth earl of Oxford. The justices agreed to hear it.

David explained his reasons for organizing the moot court:

> My original intention was that there should be a record consisting of the principal scholarly work on each side: Samuel Schoenbaum's *William Shakespeare: A Documentary Life* published in 1974, and Charlton Ogburn's *The Mysterious William Shakespeare* in 1984; that the justices would read and counsel and base their briefs and arguments solely upon these books and that the Justices would decide which side was more persuasive. But obviously, this was not done. The briefs ranged far afield and cited dozens of authorities.
>
> In my view, the proceedings offered sustenance to both sides. The orthodox position, firmly established in Academe and almost universally accepted by the general public, was strengthened by the unanimous decision of the justices that

INSPIRING LEGACY

the case presented for Oxford had not met the requisite burden of proof. At the same time, considerable encouragement of the Oxfordian case was forthcoming in the *obiter dicta* [an incidental expression of opinion made by a judge that is not essential to the decision or in establishing a precedent]. Two of the justices had made such remarks.

Those listening to the moot court learned about Oxford's life, much of it reflected in the Shakespeare plays. As a noble of ancient lineage, he was raised in the *milleu* of the royal court and expected to serve as a courtier. He studied with England's greatest scholars, who also had tutored Queen Elizabeth I. When his father died, he became a royal ward in the home of Lord Burghley, where he had access to a vast library of books on many subjects, some of them yet to be translated into English, while others were written in languages in which he was fluent. He wrote and shared his poetry, music, and dance with Queen Elizabeth I while serving as Lord Great Chamberlain.

In contrast, there is no record that a young boy named William Shakespeare ever attended his local school. What we do know is that as an adult, he was a grain merchant and tanner who signed his name several different ways, as Shagsper, Shaxper, Shaksper, or Shakspere. His wife and children were illiterate, and he left no books in his will. None of his neighbors acknowledged him as a playwright. There is no evidence that the man from Stratford ever fought in a war or traveled to Italy, the setting of so many Shakespeare plays.

Orphaned by his father's untimely death, Oxford was deeply grieved at his mother's hasty remarriage to the man he suspected of being the murderer. At twelve, he was sent to London as a royal ward to live under the guardianship of Sir William Cecil, a commoner who had risen to become an advisor to Queen Elizabeth I. Cecil nullified the original marriage contract Oxford's father had arranged with another noble family and married off his own daughter to the royal ward. The marriage permitted Cecil's elevation to the title of Lord Burghley before the wedding to equalize his noble status with that of his new son-in-law; otherwise, the marriage could not have taken place. In doing this, Cecil went against his own written opinion that early marriages for young girls were unacceptable. Nevertheless, in 1571, he married his fifteen-year-old daughter to twenty-one-year-old Oxford, but because of the bride's tender age, consummation was delayed for several years.

In 1575, the Queen granted Oxford permission to travel to Italy, France, and Germany for one year. His pregnant wife Anne was unable to accompany him. During his absence, he learned that Anne had given birth, but because eleven months had passed and he distrusted Burghley's announcement, he was sure Anne had committed adultery and that he was not the father of her child. Enraged, he returned to England and refused to live with her. He began a love affair with a Catholic lady who bore his illegitimate son and named it after him, perhaps because he had promised to marry her after divorcing his adulterous wife.

When the Queen discovered this, she locked up Oxford, his mistress, and their newborn in the Tower. Then, to protect the Protestant throne and appease Lord Burghley for the sake of his unfortunate daughter, the Queen forced Oxford to reconcile with Anne. Infuriated, his mistress's family attacked Oxford numerous times in the streets, vendetta style. He was stabbed in the leg, and the wound left him disabled. Add to this that Oxford was captured by pirates and held for ransom, and that a shipwreck left him deeply indebted to a moneylender, and these experiences leap from his life and onto the pages of the Shakespeare plays.

After Lord Oxford's return to England in 1576, the first Elizabethan theater based on an Italian design was built on the shores of the Thames that same year. Lord Oxford, after all, had been a renowned poet, translator, and author of court masques. He was known in his day as the Italianate earl. Theater was his passion, and financing theatrical productions may have led to the depletion of his financial resources in his later years.

David described the intensity of the moot court in an article for the Spring 1988 *American University Law Review*:

> The entire day of September 25 was devoted to the presentation of arguments in the morning, the deliberation of the justices at midday, and the delivery of their individual decisions in the afternoon. The event received widespread publicity in newspapers, television, and radio both in this country and abroad. The debate and decisions did not settle the controversy and were not expected to do so. But they served to focus the public attention on the issue of authorship as a choice between Stratford and Oxford, encouraging further study and research and stimulating plans for a sequel in England.

That trial's sequel took place in the Hall of the Middle Temple in London on November 26, 1988. Three law lords headed by Lord Ackner conducted a trial that drew "an impressive line-up of Queen's Counsel and expert witnesses."

Back at the original 1987 moot trial in the States, Justice Brennan declared "that the justices were at a disadvantage since none of them could possibly have delved into all of the evidence, and that without the advantage of either a judgment or a record of a lower court, we do feel just a little bit at sea."

Justice Blackmun cited the passage in *The Merchant of Venice* where Antonio is told "your mind is tossing on the sea," and observed "that's about where I find myself in trying to cipher the answer to this very fascinating issue."

Justice Stevens expressed "gnawing doubts that this great author may perhaps have been someone else." He supported an eventual retrial. "Although we agree on the ultimate outcome," he said, "the doctrine of *res judicata* [a judicial matter that has been firmly decided] does not apply."

In the matter of Shakespeare in the most common vernacular, the jury was still out. There was so much more to learn about Oxford and so little time in which to do it that the justices had no choice but to support the traditional authorship. They decided 3-0 in favor of the traditionally recognized author.

David summed up his opinion of their decision:

> While my personal inclination towards the Oxford side must be apparent, I cannot in fairness deny that the traditional view, held virtually without exception throughout Academe, has the dignity of centuries of acceptance and may well reign for many more years.
>
> I would respectfully venture the suggestion to the Stratfordians, in the spirit of Justice Steven's admonition to the Oxfordians, that the rumblings of dissent, which cannot be stilled by ignoring or deriding them, could better be dealt with by encouraging graduate students to devote research and study to bolstering the Stratfordian case in several areas of perceived inadequacy. . . . Without university training, he [the man from Stratford] would have to be a superb autodidact, learning from Ovid, Seneca, Hollingshead, Boccaccio, and Chaucer both in Latin and in English. Although no mention is made in his will of any books, they are said to

have been listed in a separate inventory, and further research may disclose books traceable as his.

The passage of the centuries should not deter further research.

Thus far, traditional Stratfordians do not even feel the need to look for such books.

Finally, concerning the Shakespeare authorship question, David wrote:

> The doubt – or heresy, as it has come to be called – was echoed and multiplied during the next century until by the 1920s, a professor at Northwestern University could list no less than 4,509 articles and books questioning or denying the Stratford authorship, a phenomenon of dissent unique in literary history.
>
> The appearance on the scene of an Elizabethan seemingly possessed of all the qualifications for the authorship of the greatest body of drama and poetry in history came as a revelation. Yet as a lawyer, I realize that the case for the Earl of Oxford, however powerful, is based largely on circumstantial evidence, as is true of the case for Stratford and indeed of many important legal decisions both civil and criminal. I felt that it may therefore be helpful to link the disciplines of the law with historical scholarship in the hope of shedding more light on the tantalizing issue of the authorship. These considerations led to my proposing and sponsoring the debate held at the Metropolitan Methodist Church in Washington on September 25, 1987 under the auspices of American University. . . .
>
> Three of the most distinguished justices of the United States Supreme Court . . . were willing to take time from their very crowded schedule to hear the debate and render

their opinions. Before them appeared two learned professors on the faculty of the Washington College of Law of The American University, Peter Jaszi for Oxford and James Boyle for Stratford. Many hours, days and weeks were spent by the learned justices and able counsel in research, study, and preparation of briefs.

But this wasn't the final verdict on the matter. In May 1998, the Lawyer's Committee of the Shakespeare Theatre of Washington conducted another Shakespeare trial with Supreme Court Justice John Paul Stevens presiding. Also in attendance were Justices William Kennedy and Ruth Bader Ginsburg, who sat on the jury.

"I first became interested in this issue when I visited Stratford many years ago and visited Shakespeare's large home," Stevens said. "Independently I was struck by the fact there were no books in the house."

At the conclusion of the trial, Stevens broke a tie vote and found in favor of Lord Oxford as the author of the Shakespeare canon.

Supreme Court justices who leaned in the direction of Oxfordian authorship were Sandra Day O'Connor and the late Antonin Scalia.

David Lloyd Kreeger's name is listed on the Shakespeare Authorship Coalition's Declaration of Reasonable Doubt (DoubtAboutWill.org), along with Charles Dickens, Walt Whitman, Mark Twain, Orson Welles, Sir Derek Jacobi, Sir Mark Rylance, Jeremy Irons, and other notables who have questioned (and continue to question) the authorship of the Stratford man.

The declaration also includes the names of former US Supreme Court Justices Harry Blackmun, Lewis Powell, and John Paul Stevens.

For more information on the seventeenth Earl of Oxford as Shakespeare, visit https://shakespeareoxfordfellowship.org.

CHAPTER 16

The Shakespeare-Oxfordian Converts: An Author's Perspective

> This book is dedicated to the late David Lloyd Kreeger, who first suggested the idea.
>
> ~ Dedication by Syril Levin Kline to Shakespeare's Changeling: A Controversial Literary Historical Novel

As a man who loved the power of words, David had been attracted to what he called "the profundity of Shakespeare's understanding of human nature in all its strengths and glory, its weaknesses and vices." He recognized the playwright's deep understanding of the law and other disciplines. At 81, he continued to be a lifelong fan of all things Shakespeare since first encountering the plays and sonnets in high school. Between 1932–1934, he had read the entire canon in pocket-sized, hardcover editions during his daily commute to and from his law office.

One summer evening in 1990, David invited me and my husband Peter to his home on Foxhall Road to discuss Shakespeare's unique genius, that it did not stem from a random act of neurons, but rather from a passion for learning that was actively nurtured by his tutors. Geniuses tend to seek out nurturing independently or are fortunate to be inspired and educated by those who recognize the gift. David wasn't sure how Peter felt about this, but Peter, author of *The Everyday Genius* and sixteen other books on education and the arts, shared that philosophy.

It was a good platform on which to start, but Peter had arrived as an authorship skeptic. David had read a great deal about the centuries-old controversy. He firmly believed that the man whose name was originally published in hyphenated form as Shake-Speare was the pseudonym of Edward DeVere, seventeenth Earl of Oxford (1550–1604), a nobleman known in his time as a scholar, poet, champion jouster, and patron of a troupe of players.

Peter told David that he had been interested in the Shakespeare authorship question during his Amherst College years and had applied to pursue his study in England, but his professors had discouraged it.

I first heard about the authorship controversy in private school. I listened intently as Peter and David good naturedly argued about the dating of the plays.

As an amateur cartoonist, one of the things that had intrigued David was the drawing of Shakespeare in the First Folio, and how its editor, Ben Jonson, cryptically challenged readers to "look not on his picture, but his book." The cartoon-like image is very different from the fine engravings of Elizabethan authors published at the time. In the First Folio, "gentle Shakespeare" seems to be hiding behind a mask.

No traditional proponent of the Stratfordian authorship has ever explained references in the plays that were found in books that had not been translated into English at the time. How could a commoner from Stratford have had access to costly foreign books, and where would he have learned the languages needed to understand them? And if the author from Stratford was illiterate, how could he have become a writer at all?

Furthermore, the depth and complexity of subjects covered in the Shakespeare plays could not have been gleaned by listening at a keyhole, eavesdropping in a pub or while taking rapid dictation as a play was going on. This laughable idea was suggested in the paperback Folger Library editions used in schools.

Delving further in Lord Oxford's biography, we read about the need for secrecy of one particular "courtly maker," a writer whose name appeared in print as far back as 1589 in *The Arte of English Poesie*:

> In Her Majesty's time that now is, are springing up another crew of Courtly makers, noblemen and gentlemen of Her Majesty's own servants who have written excellently well, as it would appear if their doings could be found out and made public with the rest, of which number is first that noble gentleman, Edward, Earl of Oxford . . . doings as I have seen . . . to deserve the highest praise . . . for comedy and interlude.

Our informative evening ended with David recommending that we read Charlton Ogburn's *The Mysterious William Shakespeare* (EPM Publications, 1984) which contains a foreword by noted historian David McCullough. "It's the only book you'll need to read on the subject," David advised. He encouraged us to write a novel about the Shakespeare authorship that would appeal to the average reader. He wondered how long such a book would take to write. Peter replied that it would take a year.

After twenty years of trial-and-error drafts, tons of research, and lots of pillow talk that Peter and I shared about Lord Oxford, my novel,

Shakespeare's Changeling, was published and dedicated to David and his son. It won a Chanticleer International First Place Chaucer award in Elizabethan/Tudor Historical Fiction and was based on the three non-fiction volumes Peter wrote about the Earl of Oxford as Shakespeare.

Over the years, Peter and I built a good-sized library of hundreds of books on the subject. We had the opportunity to meet Evelyn P. Metzger of EPM Publications in her Virginia home, and Peter received our third and special copy of *The Mysterious William Shakespeare,* personally signed by Charlton Ogburn while the two men sat with cold drinks on the front porch of Ogburn's home in Beaufort, South Carolina.

Sadly, David did not live to see the publication of *Shakespeare's Changeling.*

A few months after our visit, he passed away in November 1990.

Epilogue

The Kreeger Museum: Retrospect and Prospects

> "Art is born and takes hold wherever there is a
> timeless and insatiable longing for the spiritual."
>
> ~ Andrei Tarkovsky (1932-1986), Russian writer and filmmaker

Through a series of fortuitous events, including the growth and stabilization of GEICO over a fifteen-year period prior to his death in 1990, David and Carmen were able to successfully convert their Foxhall Road home into the Kreeger Museum, which opened to the public on June 1, 1994. Carmen's generous contributions allowed the Kreeger Museum to cultivate its numerous public programs, exhibitions, and musical presentations. She continued to contribute to other cultural institutions in the Washington, DC area until her death in 2003.

David's enduring love affair with the Washington arts community led to his embracing even more philanthropic work after his retirement. He enjoyed it immensely and was proud to inspire others to contribute as he did to almost every musical or artistic institution in the metropolitan area.

After his death, aided by the wise counsel of the Museum's board of directors, Walter Freedman, and later his son, Jay Freedman, the Kreeger Museum flourished. Under the direction of Judy Greenberg and her dedicated staff, as well as legions of outstanding docents, the Kreeger Museum ascended to new heights in the artistic community. Exhibitions by talented local artists—including Sam Gilliam, William Christenberry, John Dreyfus, and others—highlighted the early years.

Since opening its doors, the Kreeger Museum has presented over twenty-five exhibitions, including works in its permanent collection, a variety of shows highlighting Washington area artists, and presentations of works with both national and international partners and collaborators. It has offered world-class concerts and dance performances featuring local musicians as well as performers from around the globe. It has increased accessibility by expanding hours and admission policies, adding a major expansion to the Sculpture Garden, establishing new and continuing partnerships with other nonprofit organizations, and extending the impact of its innovative educational programs.

The year 2000 celebrated the performance of the Millennium Concert, initiated by Judy Greenberg and supported by the Kreeger Museum's board of directors. It was an ambitious undertaking that involved a yearlong collaboration between composer Rob Kapilow, the National Symphony Orchestra, the John F. Kennedy Center for the Performing Arts, and residents of the nation's capital. The Kreeger Museum commissioned Kapilow to compose a symphony inspired by artistic contributions from Washingtonians on the theme "DC Citypiece: Monuments at the Millennium."

Beginning in 1999, the Kreeger Museum invited residents of all ages to participate in a project entitled "Memories of the Mind and HeART: Kids Create Monuments at the Millennium." In November, Kapilow listened to their ideas, which became part of his musical "work in progress." The project gave birth to a variety of presentations that included videos, poems, essays, paintings, and sculptures by individuals, schools, and community organizations that were exhibited at various locations in the city. The Kreeger Museum also hosted an exhibition curated by Jack Rasmussen, currently director and curator of the American University Museum at the Katzen Arts Center, entitled *Remembering the Present*.

These efforts culminated in the spring of 2000 when Kapilow's composition was presented to a packed house, free and open to the public. It was performed by the National Symphony at the Kennedy Center.

Another significant milestone at the Kreeger Museum was artist William Christenberry's 2001 exhibition entitled *Changing Landscapes—The Source Revisited*. Guest curator Milena Kalinovska described Christenberry's inspiration as reflecting on "the beloved rural Southern landscape of his childhood" coupled with his "sense of duty to deal with all things difficult or tragic." In a later interview, Christenberry recalled that David "bought art because he loved it, not because of investment value, but for the softness of art and the majesty of architecture."

The Kreeger Museum's workshops for children were described in a 2006 *Washington Post* article. Artists Anthony Brock and Susan Fishel explored the qualities of nature and light. Artist Susan Hostetler used the work of Georges Braque, who sometimes blended sand and sawdust into his paintings, to inspire children to create their own works using acrylic paint, colored paper, ink, and sand. Building children's confidence in their creative abilities was paramount in her presentation. According to Fishel, the theme of the day was the idea that "great artists from the past still speak to the children, and that art is timeless."

Artist Tom Wesselmann was one of the key figures in the twentieth-century pop art movement. Before his death in 2004, he and his wife, Claire, had planned an exhibition that Wesselmann described as "a well edited selection of the best drawings available covering the full range of my varied production . . . a show that will enlarge the common perception of what drawing is to a surprising and rewarding degree." Claire curated the Kreeger Museum's 2011 exhibition entitled *Tom Wesselmann DRAWS*.

As mentioned earlier, artist Leonardo Nierman became a lifelong friend of Carmen and David, who were early supporters of his bold and colorful work. They offered him a one-man show of his paintings at their Fessenden Street home long before Philip Johnson's design for the house on Foxhall Road was a gleam in anyone's eye. Nierman's gift of the stainless-steel sculpture entitled *Flame of Friendship* graces the Kreeger Museum's Sculpture Garden along with many other outdoor works gifted by other talented artists.

The Kreeger Museum continues its mission to share art, architecture, and music through educational programs and initiatives, lectures, panel discussions, gallery talks, and exhibitions. The Conversations program reaches out to adults with dementia, offering unique experiences with art, music, and meaning.

David and Carmen made people feel comfortable in their home and wanted to make their collection available to the public. Their legacy continues to inspire on a real and spiritual level, as many visitors have often commented that it feels as if their spirits are still in the building, offering peace, serenity, and beauty. Their love of art and music as well as their dedication and devotion to sharing that love with others will continue to guide the Kreeger Museum's mission.

"As the Museum moves into the future," says Director Helen Chason, "it will continue maintaining responsible stewardship of the collection, building and grounds, sharing and supporting art, music and architecture across the city. It is continuing to provide art education to students, including those in underserved communities, and encourages partnerships across a multitude of sectors."

Exciting new additions to the Sculpture Garden are the Woodland Garden expansion and walking paths. The recent plantings and cultivation of this outdoor space were added in 2021 with the oversight and coordination of Ineke Kreeger. The meandering paths create a pastoral extension of the galleries into the peaceful charm of this natural setting.

The Kreeger Museum offers free Saturday afternoon programs in the galleries and garden, including visitors from across the city and globe, making the collection accessible to all. It will continue to collaborate with sister arts institutions in the city, the United States, and abroad, and to create opportunities for regional artists to share their talent.

"We look forward to the years ahead, building on the successes of our past and setting out on new ventures as we reach across the city to share art, music and architecture," says Chason.

Appendix

Barnet Kreeger's Zava'ah—Jewish Ethical Will

Barnet Kreeger passed away on January 3, 1974. He left behind a letter written in Yiddish for his children, which was found among the papers on his desk at the home of his daughter Shirley and her husband, Louis A. Mezey, with whom he lived from 1951 to 1969 in Miami, Florida.

The letter was translated into English by Barnet's niece Marion Storm of the Bronx, New York, the daughter of Barnet's brother, Nathan Krugler. It was composed in the form of a *zava'ah* (Jewish ethical will) and demonstrates the spiritual values of a man steeped in learning, kindness, and generosity, values that he modeled for his children during his lifetime and set down as advice for future generations.

> One cannot foresee the future or its various occurrences—many times unforeseen and unexpected—therefore do I desire and expect the following from my dear children—my daughter Shirley, my son David, and my son Morris:
>
> 1. I want you all to be treated alike. Consider yourselves as one family. Equal. Do not become alienated, and impress this upon your children. That

is to say that blood, your own blood, means more than money.

2. I want to say that your father always had a strong desire to help the needy. I gave according to my circumstances, sometimes more and sometimes less. But I gave. This "habit" do I want you to inherit and take over.

3. And now, my dear children, I'd like very much if at all possible, for all of you to get together on the day of my departure from this world—once a year—do not cry—do not mourn—but lovingly and quietly get together in friendship and trust and enjoy the day. This, I believe, will bind you in love and keep you all together. Do not become alienated. This is the wish of your best friend who has done all he possibly could for his children—a task every father should do.

Your devoted father,
Barnet Kreeger

Letter from Barnet to David and Carmen, 1947

My dear children,

Received your telegram and letters and am very glad to hear you are all well. This is the most important thing that I want to hear. I am also glad to hear that the law practice is good, and you don't have to depend on the stock market. If it can come down from 67 to 40, it could come down from 40 to 20, but I think none of us has to worry about it, as long as we are healthy, so we'll always make a living.

And about the home, I am going to tell you what I told Lou and Shirley. The landlord will not dispossess you. So amen, you'll stay where you are, and everyone should try to pay off the bank lease you'll own, and healthier you will be. Less worry, more health.

And don't forget you promised me that you will take it easy, that you would not work so hard. You write that you have to work in the night. I don't like it at all. You took in Ragland as a partner, so you should not work so hard. When you are busy, put more help on. I don't say take more cases or take all you can, but put more help on. Don't forget, you are not any more a "boyele" [little boy] you are a responsible family man, and health you can't buy for millions.

You can see it right now on Carolita, God bless her, and a few years later you have to think about her marriage, and then it is not far from you being "a zayde" [grandfather] and Carmen "a bubbe" [grandmother]. Tell you the truth, I would like to see it. But take care of your health and Carmen's health so the children will be better off in every way.

You know, Sonny dear, your estimate that five years later when the stock will rise to this and that point, I will be worth a million dollars, reminds me that 55 years ago, I read a novel from a Russian writer.

A farmer goes hunting, and walking through the woods, he sees a rabbit behind a tree, so he slows down his steps and he stands to figure, if I only can catch him alive and get another one, these two should bring in five more rabbits, and the five will bring twenty more, and the twenty will bring in one hundred rabbits. And when I sell the one hundred rabbits, look at the money I'll get! And he was so happy that he could not control his happiness, and he screamed, "Gosh!" and scared the rabbit away so far that even his rifle could not get him. What I say, Sonny, is this—it is better a live rabbit than a dead lion.

I "pachke" [elaborate] on too much.

I'm feeling very good so far and give my best to Carmen and children, and I wish you all a Happy New Year.

With love and kisses, your Dad and Pop

P.S.—About the books, I would suggest that you should not spend any money now because Sholem Aleichem's books I have. So what kind of Jewish books you could get in Washington? And if you want I could get 'em all over, so better save the money.

With love,
Pop

Speaking a Common Language

In the 1930s, David learned Spanish in Puerto Rico so that he could speak to Carmen's mother. It would never have occurred to him then that one day in 1982, he would use it to speak with visiting royalty. He told the following story:

> When the King and Queen of Spain came here for a visit, a group of us from the American Jewish Committee had an audience with King Juan Carlos to thank him for his interest in synagogues and their legitimization for the first time in Spain since the expulsion of Jews in 1492.
>
> I spoke to him in Spanish, and he asked where I had learned it.
>
> "I learned it in Puerto Rico so I could speak to my mother-in-law," I replied.

"I had an even harder time than you did. I had to learn Greek to speak to Queen Sofia's mother," the King said.

I had the temerity to ask, "Well, how did you court the Queen?"

"I courted her in English," the King replied, "because Sofia knew English. I didn't know Greek and she didn't know Spanish. English was our common language."

That night there was a dinner in their honor at the Spanish Embassy. As Carmen and I went through the receiving line, we greeted the royal couple. The Queen had not been at the afternoon reception because the audience had been just for the men, so this was the first time I was meeting her. As we went through the line, the King exclaimed to his wife, "Here is the gentleman who had to learn Spanish so he could talk to his mother-in-law!" And they both laughed.

This was a common bond between us.

Telford Taylor's Remarks at the Nuremburg Trials

David Kreeger and Telford Taylor were classmates at Harvard Law School. Taylor was one of the prosecutors at the Nuremberg Trials. These are a few of his remarks. David believed strongly in his message:

> The indictment accuses these men of major responsibility for visiting upon mankind the most searing and catastrophic war in modern history. It accuses them of wholesale enslavement, plunder, and murder. The crimes with which these men are charged were not committed in rage or under the stress of sudden temptation. They were not the slips or lapses of otherwise well-ordered men. One does not build a

stupendous war machine in a fit of passion, nor an Auschwitz factory during a passing spasm of brutality.

What these men did was done with the utmost deliberation and would, I venture to surmise, be repeated if the opportunity should recur. There will be no mistaking the ruthless purposefulness with which the defendants embarked upon their course of conduct. That purpose was to turn the German nation into a military machine and build it into an engine of destruction so terrifyingly formidable that Germany could, by brutal threats and, if necessary, by war, impose her will and her dominion on Europe and later on other nations beyond the seas.

In this arrogant and supremely criminal adventure, the defendants were eager and leading participants.

David's Patent Case
(In his own words)

Only one or two government agencies asserted ownership of patents though government employees in government laboratories were designing and inventing. It was a rather careless policy. There was a law that was passed in the early part of the Twentieth century, which said that when a government employee developed an invention and patented it during his term of employment, the government was entitled to a full license to use the invention in its laboratories without having to pay a royalty to the employee/inventor. That was an actual statute.

But in practice, most of the agencies let the employee keep title to the patent and he could license it to anybody on the outside and keep the royalties, even though it had been made on government time and had been completely paid for by the government.

In the Pentagon, in the Department of Defense (which was then called Department of the Navy and Department of War) they would also let their research contractors keep the patents. For example, the department would engage a manufacturing company with a research department to develop a better propeller blade or some safety equipment for an airplane. The Department would tell them the results it wanted the company to meet, and the government would pay for everything including the overhead of the contractor, its profit and so on. Then the contractor would bring out a device and a development that it could patent, and all the government would take would be a license to use it and the contractor would then be able to exploit the invention financially for his own benefit.

The patent was issued in the name of the inventor, but it was assigned to the corporation for whom the research employee had worked. This was unlike the government practice where the government employee's invention would be patented in the name of the employee rather than in the name of the United States, and generally would not be assigned to the government.

But if you worked for General Motors and the government made a contract with the company to develop an improvement on the automobile parts or on a motor that was being used by the Pentagon, General Motors would own that patent because it had a contract with the employee that all patents be assigned to the corporation.

It seemed to me that this was in the area of proprietary rights; that this was a matter of who is entitled to the benefits of the work being done at government instigation, government financing and government control, and that all of the benefits would belong to the government and not just a non-exchange license.

I didn't feel that it was appropriate for an engineer who was assigned to do research to make a fortune out of the results of what he did for the government in the course of his employment; whereas another engineer who was not assigned to that area of research but might be assigned to some equally important aspect of engineering or science and who did just as valuable work for the government, to have nothing comparable to this bonanza that the inventor would have.

I thought it ought to belong to the government, and the same was true of inventions made by government contractors. I did not see that in anyway inconsistent with civil liberties.

On the other hand, if the man were to invent the device on the outside, that would be another matter. You get a thin line there if he invented it after he left the government, the extent to which he utilized some advantages that he got in the government after he leaves.

We have that in conflict-of-interest situations where a government employee develops special information or expertise while dealing with huge corporations, and then next year he leaves the government and goes with that huge corporation, and to what extent did the prospect of employment affect his work there. There are some gray areas.

David Lloyd Kreeger's 75th Birthday Celebration (1984)

A tribute by Yvonne Levi Kushner

This is a tribute to Carmen and David Kreeger upon his 75th birthday.

Pearl Bailey used to sing a song that began "Elegance, ya gotta have elegance." Well, this gentleman has elegance, not just the sartorial kind, but in that is no slouch, make no mistake. His is a different type of elegance, elegance of a searching intellectual mind and brilliant epic taste, such as had Renaissance doges and princes, men of culture and great estate.

Now our man is a modern prince, a perfectionist who does things right. He has a cult for the beauty and the bravery of life. By his gifts, he redeems us from the mundane trials of everyday living, making life more meaningful in many ways. Oh, his gifts are manifold! One cannot ably or completely detail this generous giving. Yes, he bountifully shares of his treasures and his work with you and with me. Happily, he plans for us—and remember, it's all free.

Take for instance those treasures on the walls of their Foxhall home. Whenever the doors are open wide, you feel the wonder of their beauty as you walk quietly about inside. The house itself enfolds you into itself. The warmth and kindliness of the greeting there reaches out to you—hospitality beyond compare. One's spirit is lifted by this house. All is in perfect proportion, in harmony all things blend, completing its magnificent creative design. Oh, it fills one's heart with a sense of peace while pleasuring the eye and mystifying the mind. Only once before have I had such a feeling, and it was in another man's gift to the world, in Vence in the Chapel by Matisse.

There again, individual creations result in an exquisite unity, creating a quiet calm and a sense of lovely ease.

We thank you, Carmen and David, for all the treasures. But for me, I'm most grateful for the theater. There in the theater, our thoughts are mingled with the ancient texts and universally revealed truths, the mores and customs of times gone by. Poetry and prose fall equally on receptive ears. Modern, ultra-modern staccato ideas engage our feelings as communication between players and audience fuses into a personal understanding and an experience across the footlights.

There is a radiant magic about you, David. Ah, but you're not the magician—oh, no, no. The magician is the beautiful gracious Senora who stands by your side, complementing your shadow with complete understanding of your ideas and devoted love in her eyes.

And now to end this sincere tribute, I give you the same toast made years ago: to Carmen and David, who dreamt that they dwelled in carpeted halls and made that dream come true. Their artistic masters look down on these two, recognizing them as kindred masters - masters of art, music, dance, finance, giving.

To the Kreegers—who have mastered the greatest art of all—the art of living.

Gratitude and Acknowledgments

As author, first and foremost, I greatly appreciate having worked closely with Eloise Pelton, who served as the Kreeger Museum's archivist since 2004. Eloise was instrumental in helping me access documents that included speeches, photos, articles, and the love letters exchanged between David and Carmen before their marriage. Her familiarity with their lives, interests, and activities demonstrates her devotion to the museum and to the Kreeger family.

Special thanks to the Kreeger Museum's Director Helen Chason and to Collection and Private Events Manager Joanna Baker for their vast knowledge of the masterpieces in the museum; and to Basil Arendse and all the Kreeger Museum staff who made me feel at home while I worked on this project.

Thank you to my friends and colleagues Carol Webster, Regina Williams, A.F. Winter and Shari Stauch of Main Street Writes in Summerville, South Carolina, for their comments on earlier drafts, and to my late husband Peter Kline who will always serve as my literary muse.

Over the years, many volunteer docents lent their time and energies to conduct visitors through the museum. Their knowledge and dedication contributed to the daily operations of the Kreeger Museum over the years and were a great inspiration to me.

Heartfelt thanks to Carol Ingall, Bob Davis, Ineke Kreeger, and so many others who read early drafts of this book, offered suggestions, and most importantly asked significant questions.

And finally, sincere gratitude to Peter Kreeger for his guidance, assistance, and chapter-by-chapter editing, and for his active collaboration and full support of this project.

Photo Gallery

Barnett Kreeger, 1965

Carmen and David greet cellist Pablo Cassals, 1971

David's 80th Birthday Celebration, 1989

An abiding friendship: David with Mstislav Rostropovich, 1989

David with dear friend Isaac Stern, 1989

David and Isaac Stern play Mozart's "upside down" Duetto, which allows two violinists to face each other while performing, 1989

David with friends Isaac Stern and Mstislav Rostropovich, 1989

Carmen and David's wedding portrait, San Juan, Puerto Rico, 1938

David and Carmen, Washington, DC, 1945

David and Carmen loved to dance, 1982

Carmen in Fessenden St. home, Washington, DC, 1967

Carmen and David with Justice William O. Douglas and his wife Cathy, 1975

Carmen and David with Indiana Senator Birch Bayh and his wife Marvella, 1975

David and Carmen, 1978

David at National Symphony Orchestra Gala, 1978

David and Carmen, 1975

News clipping announcing David's scholarship to Harvard Law School, 1929

Carmen's family: Rafaela (seated) with Marina, Kiki and Carmen; Dr. Matanzo with Frank and Rosita, 1918

Laura Kreeger with her children David, Morris and Shirley, 1915

Carmen and David with friends Austin and Gogo Kiplinger, 1982

David with niece Laura Sandberg and husband Tom

David, age 15, Summer 1923

David age 20, 1929

Wedding portrait of Carmen and David, San Juan, Puerto Rico, 1938

David and Carmen in the Mallorca home of artist Joan Miró and his wife Pilar for Miró's 80th birthday

Carmen with daughter Carolita in Arlington, VA, 1942

About the Author

Syril Levin Kline is the recipient of a First Place International Chanticleer Book award for *Shakespeare's Changeling: A Controversial Literary Historical Novel*. She coauthored *The Butterfly Dreams* with her late husband Peter Kline. Her career as an educator, actress, musician, and theater director underscores her passion for the arts. Syril's work as a journalist influenced her reporting for the history of David and Carmen Kreeger's appreciation and support of the arts in Washington, DC, and around the world.

Index

A

Abt, John, 43
Adams, John, 135
Aesop, 103
African art, 130–131
Agnew, Spiro T., 120
Agricultural Adjustment
    Administration (AAA), 41,
    43–45
Amory, Cleveland, 125
Anderson, Marian, 93
Anschluss, 87
anti-Semitism, 34–37
Arena Stage, 94
Arendse, Basil, 163
Arrabal (Nierman), 117
art collection
    at Fessenden Street house, 108–118
    at Foxhall Road house, 123–134
art history at Rutgers University, 25–27
The Arte of English Poesie, 145
"As You Like It," 135
atomic bombs dropped on Japan, 90
atrium garden in Foxhall Road house,
    126–128

B

Baker, Joanna, 163
Barnes, Albert C., 27
Barnes Foundation, 27
Beale, Joey, 40
The Beautiful and Damned
    (Fitzgerald), 61
Berkshire Hathaway, 121–122
Blackmun, Harry, 136, 140, 142
Boyle, James, 142
Braque, Georges, 149
Brennan, William, 136, 139
Brice, Fanny, 54
Brock, Anthony, 149
Brown, J. Carter, 108
Buffet, Warren, 121–122
Byrd, Walter D., 109–110
Byrne, John "Jack," 121–122

C

Cagney, James, 87
Capricho (Nierman), 116
Carnegie Hall, 111
Carson, Clarence B., 90
cartoons, drawing, 18–19, 24–25

casualties in World War II, 90
Cecil, William (Lord Burghley), 137–138
Changing Landscapes—The Source Revisited (Christenberry), 149
character, building, 14–22
Chardon, Carlos, 45
Chason, Helen, 150–151, 163
Cheshire, Maxine, 129
child rearing, 14–22
Christenberry, William, 148, 149
College Humor, 25
Constitution Hall, 93
Constitutional law at Rutgers University, 29
Corcoran Gallery of Art, 94
Cott, Perry, 114
Court of Appeals of New Jersey, 39–40
courtship of David and Carmen Kreeger, 48–59
critical thinking, importance of, 23–24, 32
cultural arts in Washington, DC, during and after New Deal, 92–96

D

Davidson, Lorimer "Davy," 106–107, 110, 120–121
Davis, Bob, 164
deaths in World War II, 90
debt collection, 103–104
DeVere, Edward (seventeenth Earl of Oxford), 136–142, 144–145
Dewey, John, 27
Dickens, Charles, 31, 142
Dobson, Gwen, 124
Dorra, Henri, 108
Douglass, Frederick, 130
Dreyfus, John, 148

E

Eckhardt, Wolf von, 126–127
education
    in childhood, 14–22
    importance of, 23–24
    at Rutgers University, 23–30
Elementos (Nierman), 117
Elizabeth I (queen), 137–138
Emerson, Ralph Waldo, 123
European vacation (1937), 53, 60–68, 87
Evans, Maurice, 54

F

farmers, 43–45
Federal Art Project, 92–93
Federal Communications Commission, 96
Federal Employees Ambulance Campaign Committee, 87
Feigen, Richard, 111
Fessenden Street house, 109–110
Fischer, Louis, 86
Fishel, Susan, 149
Fitzgerald, F. Scott, 60–61
Flame of Friendship (Nierman), 150
Ford, Gerald R., 120
Forrest, Faith, 18
Forrest, Sidney, 18
Fortas, Abe, 18
Foster, Richard, 123, 132–134

Foxhall Road house, 123–134
Franco, Francisco, 78
Frank, Jerome, 43
Frankfurter, Felix, 98–99
Freedman, Jay, 147
Freedman, Walter, 147
Freud, Sigmund, 136
Friends of Spanish Democracy, 79, 86
Friends of the Abraham Lincoln Brigade, 87
"full faith and credit," 39–40
furniture in Foxhall Road house, 129

G

galitzianer, 55
gallega, 55
garden in Foxhall Road house, 126–128
Garfield, James, 95
GEICO (Government Employees Insurance Company)
    art collection made possible by, 110–111
    investment in, 104–107
    management changes in, 120–122
Getlein, Frank, 125–126
Gilbert, William S., 31
Gilliam, Sam, 148
Ginsburg, Ruth Bader, 142
Gone with the Wind (Mitchell), 54
Goodwin, Leo, 106
Graham, Ben, 106, 107
Graham, Martha, 69
Graves, Olga R., 124
Great Depression, 88
Greenberg, Judy, 148

Gruening, Ernest, 45

H

Haber, Leonard, 67
Harvard Law School, 30, 32–35
Hellman, Lillian, 87
Hemingway, Ernest, 86
Hendry, Helen, 128
Hindenburg disaster, 54
Hirohito (emperor of Japan), 90
Hitler, Adolph, 86, 87, 88
Hostetler, Susan, 149
Hughes, Langston, 87

I

Ickes, Harold, 93
immigration, 88–89
Ingall, Carol Kreeger, v, 96, 111, 164
Ingall, David, v
Irons, Jeremy, 136, 142

J

Jacobi, Derek, 142
Jacobs, Nat, 37–38
Japan, atomic bombs dropped on, 90
Jaramillo y Lago, Rafaela, 51, 55, 75, 76
Jaszi, Peter, 142
Jefferson Memorial, 95
Jews
    anti-Semitism in law firms, 34–37
    Kristallnacht, 89
    Nuremberg Laws of 1935, 88
John F. Kennedy Center for the Performing Arts, 94, 148
Johnson, Hugh, 90

Johnson, Lyndon B., 119
Johnson, Philip, 123–134
Jonniaux, Alfred, 115
Jonson, Ben, 144
Judicial Conference of Senior Judges of the Courts of Appeals, 40

K

Kalinovska, Milena, 149
Kapilow, Rob, 148, 149
Kasen, Dan, 53, 60–68, 76, 87
Kennedy, Jacqueline, 94
Kennedy, John F., 94, 119
Kennedy, Robert F., 119, 132
Kennedy, William, 142
Kent State University, 119
King, Martin Luther, Jr., 119, 132
Kiplinger, Austin, 94
Kirk, William, 27–28
Kline, Peter Lee, 23, 143–146, 163
Kline, Syril Levin, 143–146
Koussevitzky, Serge, 30
Kreeger (Krugler), Barnet, 1–13, 23, 75
    birth of children, 11–12
    blessing of David's marriage, 54–55, 76
    children's accomplishments, 12–13
    David's letters about real estate, 100–101
    escape to London, 5–6
    father's death, 2
    illness of child, 12
    legal issues in New York, 8–11
    marriage of, 11
    military conscription, 4–5
    parenting skills, 14–22
    pushcart business, 6–8
    sale of grocery store, 19–20
    wife's death, 21–22
Kreeger, Carmen (Matanzo), 13
    art collection, 108–118
    courtship with David, 48–59
    dancing, 70–71
    daughter Carol's birth, 96
    education, 51, 69
    family background, 51, 55
    Fessenden Street house, 109–110
    first home purchase, 100
    Foxhall Road house, 123–134
    legacy of, 147–151
    piano purchase, 95
    portrait sitting, 115
    South American Olympics, 71–72
    Spanish Civil War (1936-1939) opinions, 80, 84–85
    Venezuela vacation (1936), 70
    Washington, DC, philanthropy, 94
    wedding of, 59, 72–76
Kreeger, David Lloyd
    AAA employment, 43–45
    accomplishments of, 13
    art collection, 108–118
    birth of, 12, 16
    civilian service during World War II, 89
    courtship with Carmen, 48–59
    dancing with Carmen, 70–71
    daughter Carol's birth, 96
    death of, 146
    debt collection, 103–104
    drawing cartoons, 18–19, 24–25

early education, 14–22
European vacation (1937), 53, 60–68, 87
Fessenden Street house, 109–110
fiftieth birthday, 118
first home purchase, 100
Foxhall Road house, 123–134
GEICO investment, 104–107
GEICO management changes, 120–122
law school and early legal career, 31–41
legacy of, 147–151
moot court on Shakespeare authorship, 136–142
mother's death, 21–22
music lessons, 17
piano purchase, 95
PRRA employment, 45–47
real-estate investments, 101
Rutgers University education, 23–30
school report card, 18–19
Shakespeare conversations with Peter Kline, 143–146
Spanish Civil War (1936-1939) opinions, 78–87
stage fright, 20–21
steting FDR, 99–100
Time magazine letters, 80–83
U.S. Supreme Court arguments, 96–99
Washington, DC, employment, 92–102
wedding of, 59, 72–76
Kreeger, Ineke, v, 151, 164

Kreeger, Laura (Betensky), 11–12, 14–22, 23
Kreeger, Morris, 12–13, 14, 15, 16, 76
Kreeger, Peter, v, 109, 111, 164
Kreeger Museum, 147–151, 163. *See also* Foxhall Road house
Kristallnacht, 89
Krugler, Harris, 4
Krugler, Nathan, 4
Krugler, Sheine Feige, 2–5

L

legal training
    Constitutional law class at Rutgers, 29
    critical thinking and, 23–24, 32
    David Kreeger's early legal career, 31–41
    Roman law class at Rutgers, 28
Leigh, Vivien, 113
Levitt, Adolph, 113
Longfellow, Henry Wadsworth, 119

M

MacLeish, Archibald, 87
Main Street Writes, 163
Matanzo, Carmen. *See* Kreeger, Carmen (Matanzo)
Matanzo y Gonzalez, Francisco, 51, 55
McCarthy, Joseph, 43
McCullough, David, 145
Mellon, Andrew W., 95
"Memories of the Mind and HeART: Kids Create Monuments at the Millennium," 148
Meshekoff, Edward, 133–134

Messetti, Jesse, 101
Metzger, Evelyn P., 146
Mezey, Freddie, 13, 53
Mezey, Louis A., 13
Mezey, Shirley (Kreeger), 11, 13, 14, 15, 16
Millennium Concert, 148
Mitchell, Margaret, 54
moot court on Shakespeare authorship, 135–142
Morrow, Samuel, 128–129, 132
Morse, Earl, 113–114, 131
Morse, Irene, 113
Munro, Thomas, 25–27, 115
Museum of African Art, 130
music
    childhood lessons, 17, 20–21
    Millennium Concert, 148
    piano purchase by David and Carmen, 95
    pleasure of, 112–113
    at Rutgers University, 25
    Stradivarius violins, 111–112
The Mysterious William Shakespeare (Ogburn), 136, 145

N

National Archives, 95
National Gallery of Art, 95, 114
National Museum of African Art, 130
National Symphony Orchestra, 93, 94, 148
National Theater, 93–94
New Deal, 39, 41, 42, 88, 90, 92–94
Nierman, Leonardo, 116–118, 150
Nixon, Richard M., 119–120

North American Committee to Aid Spain, 87
Nuremberg Laws of 1935, 88
Nuremberg Trials, 91

O

O'Connor, Sandra Day, 142
Odiorne, Louise, 126–127
Ogburn, Charlton, 136, 145
Oxford, seventeenth earl of. *See* DeVere, Edward (seventeenth Earl of Oxford)

P

The Paper Chase, 33
parenting skills, 14–22
parking meters in Washington, DC, 95
patents, 99
Pearl Harbor bombing, 89
Pelton, Eloise, 163
Platt, Adele, 132
political cartoons in San Juan, 47
Pope, John Russell, 95
Powell, Lewis, 142
Pressman, Lee, 43
Puerto Rico Reconstruction Administration (PRRA), 45–47

Q

"Quiereme Mucho," 48

R

Ragland, Rawlings, 47, 49, 101
Rasmussen, Jack, 149

Remembering the Present (Rasmussen), 149
Richard III, 54
RMS *Aquitania*, 65
RMS *Berengaria*, 60–61, 68
Robbins, Warren, 130–131
Rock Creek Park, 109–110
Roman law at Rutgers University, 28
Roosevelt, Eleanor, 93
Roosevelt, Franklin D., 42, 92
    American isolationism, 88–89
    death of, 90
    election of, 39
    portrait painting, 115
    Steinway & Sons piano, 95
    steting by David Kreeger, 99–100
Roosevelt, Theodore, 124
Rostropovich, Mstislav, 30
Ruinas (Nierman), 116
Rutgers Chanticleer, 24–25
Rutgers University, 23–30
Rylance, Mark, 142

S

Sandburg, Carl, 87
Scalia, Antonin, 142
Schoenbaum, Samuel, 136
segregation in Washington, DC, 93–94
Shakespeare, William
    David Kreeger and Peter Kline conversation about, 143–146
    moot court on authorship, 135–142

Shakespeare Authorship Coalition's Declaration of Reasonable Doubt, 142
Shakespeare's Changeling (Kline), 146
Shapiro, Bernie, 101
sharecroppers, 43–45
Shea, Francis, 43, 45–46, 96
Sheehan, Vincent, 86
Sidwell Friends School, 110
Simpson, Lou, 121
Sinclair, Upton, 87
Smith, Ed, 45
Socratic inquiry, 24
Solomon Brothers, 121
South American Olympics, 71–72
Spanish Civil War (1936-1939), 78–87
"splashing in" the New Year, 75–76
staircase in Foxhall Road house, 133–134
Stalin, Joseph, 78
Steinway & Sons, 95
Stern, Isaac, 30, 111
Stevens, John Paul, 136, 140, 142
Stone, Harlan Fiske, 97
Stradivari, Antonio, 111–112
Stradivarius violins, 111–112

T

Tarkovsky, Andrei, 147
Taylor, Telford, 43, 77, 91
Time magazine, 80–83, 86
Tom Wesselmann DRAWS, 150
Twain, Mark, 60, 135, 142

U

U.S. Supreme Court, 96–99

V

van Gogh, Vincent, 114
Vase with Flowers (van Gogh), 114
Vietnam War, 119

W

WACS (Women's Army Corps), 89
Walstrom, John, 47, 49, 50
The War of the Worlds (Wells), 96
Washington, DC, cultural arts during and after New Deal, 92–96
Washington Opera, 94
Washington Performing Arts Society, 94
Watergate, 120
WAVES (Women Accepted for Voluntary Emergency Service), 89
Welles, Orson, 96, 142
Wells, H.G., 96
Wesselmann, Claire, 149–150
Wesselmann, Tom, 149–150
WETA-TV, 94
Whitman, Walt, 142
William Shakespeare: A Documentary Life (Schoenbaum), 136
World War I veterans' benefits, 38
World War II, 87–91

Z

Ziegfeld Follies, 54
Zukerman, Pinchas, 30

www.ingramcontent.com/pod-product-compliance
Lightning Source LLC
Chambersburg PA
CBHW071238070526
44583CB00017B/2242